ABOUT THE A

Sir Frank Fox was born in Australia in 1874. He was a journalist, author, war correspondent and campaigner. This was his first book published in 1903 with illustrations from his friend, and Australia's most important artist, Norman Lindsay. The two worked together at the Australian monthly literary magazine The Lone Hand.

In 1914 he was attached to the Belgian army during the German invasion. In view of his experiences in that conflict he longed to become a combatant and was commissioned into the British Army in December 1914. Posted to France, Fox was blown up during the Battle of the Somme and suffered severe injuries. During his convalescence in England he worked for MI7 but contrived to be posted to Haig's GHQ in Montreuil-sur-Mer in the run up to the final offensive against Germany. He was appointed O.B.E. (Military) and was Mentioned in Despatches. Fox was a prolific author writing 5 books relating to World War One including "GHQ Montreuil-sur-Mer" during his service. In 1922 he accompanied George V and Lord Haig to the military cemeteries in Belgium and France and wrote an account in "The King's Pilgrimage", shortly to be republished.

Beaumont Fox
00 44 (0)2076290981
www.sirfrankfox.com

BREAKER MORANT - BUSHMAN
AND BUCCANEER

Harry Morant: His 'Ventures and Verses

WITH MANY ILLUSTRATIONS, AND
A MAP SHOWING THE BUSHVELDT
CARBINEERS' OPERATIONS;

is the earliest record of Breaker
Morant´s exploits and reprinted for the first
time since 1902. Written under the
pseudonym of Frank Renar by Frank Fox,
it provides a vivid account of the Boer War
with drawings by Norman Lindsay.
The front cover image is "Shoot straight…"
By Norman Lindsay (1879-1969) depicting
the scene immortalized in the Oscar no-
minated Beresford film of 1980. The iconic
image is available as a poster on
www.sirfrankfox.com

PUBLISHERS NOTE: Most of the Verses
herein published first saw print in THE
BULLETIN, one or two in the WINDSOR
AND RICHMOND GAZETTE and
THE WORLD'S NEWS.

In compiling the history of Morant, the
author has had the use of a great mass of
private manuscripts, and the kindness of
those lending them is here acknowledged.
Most of the illustrations are from authentic
photographs.

BREAKER MORANT - BUSHMAN AND BUCCANEER

Harry "The Breaker" Morant

BUSHMAN AND BUCCANEER

Harry Morant: His ´Ventures and Verses

FRANK RENAR
(SIR FRANK FOX)

Beaumont Fox
2017

BREAKER MORANT - BUSHMAN AND BUCCANEER
Harry Morant: His ´Ventures and Verses
by Sir Frank Fox

2nd Edition, First Published by H. T. Dunn & Co.,
Queen's Place. Sydney 1902

ISBN 978-0-9928901-4-8

Beaumont Fox, 37 St. James's Place, London SW1A 1NS
02076290981
www.sirfrankfox.com

FOREWORD

It is an extraordinary thing that 115 years after his death by firing squad, Breaker Morant's life and fate continue to excite controversy.

The seminal work about him was written by Frank Fox (under a pseudonym) in "Breaker Morant - Bushman and Buccaneer" published in 1902. This was the only contemporary account of Morant's exploits.

Fox was on the staff of the Sydney Bulletin, and presumably came to know of Morant through their mutual friendship with Andrew Barton "Banjo" Paterson, the composer of Waltzing Matilda.

Something of a Buccaneer himself in print, on a horse (the artist Norman Lindsay described him as "an equine exhibitionist") and in battle, Fox's portraits of the time reflect a curious affinity with that of Morant, and of their mutual interests.

Fox's book was the basis of the play by Kenneth Ross, and later the highly successful film made by the Australian producer Bruce Beresford in 1980.

Morant's story is essentially a romantic one. Who would not love the account of a roistering horseman, drinker and womaniser in the Australian Outback?

This alone would be enough for a drama, let alone his obscure past, his compulsive versifying, and his unorthodox military exploits in a war of the British Empire.

However, the myth persists, and only now have researchers in England uncovered some of the truth.

His declared origins have been debunked, as have accusations that his trial by Court Martial was conducted unfairly. The latter cause is still being pursued in Australia by those pressing for a posthumous pardon.

Not only was Morant of humbler stock than he maintained, but his outlandish conduct in South Africa during the Boer War seems to have been judged in proper and orthodox fashion.

Australian attempts to justify his actions apparently no longer stand the test.

Despite this, nothing can take away the daredevil image of the charming, reckless and brave man whose ventures and verses have kept his memory alive for over a Century.

Dr.Charles Goodson-Wickes

Dr.Charles Goodson-Wickes is Sir Frank Fox's great-grandson and his Literary Executor.

AUTHOR'S FOREWORD.

O F the chequered career, and most unhappy death of Harry Morant, I purpose to set forth the true facts, without word of comment. Let those who will think of the trusty friend, the daring rider, the man of great boldness to meet his death; and those who will of the asvogels hovering over stark bodies of Boer farmers, killed not in fair chance of war and heat of sturdy battle, but most ignobly in cold after-thought. Some, 1 trow, will give to Harry Morant a shudder of pity, as to a brave man who died, mistakenly avenging his friend and serving his country; others—in their minds the horror of those dark murders of patriots holding back an invader from their hearths, and an enemy from their babes—will look on his end with grim content. It will not be my task to sit in judgment, but to give with all faithfulness the sorry history of the man, withholding nothing of fact, venturing nothing of censure or apology.

FRANK RENAR.

HARRY MORANT - BUSHMAN

THE men of Devon have aye been doughty to fight, and reckless withal, caring little for the shedding of their own blood—less for that of others. And in the days of England's stress-when an enemy's ships hovered around her coast, or St. George's banner was upheld against desperate odds on the fields of France, or the Spanish King had to be met on the Main—this dour quality of Devon men was of no light value. So can witness many a Drake, Prideaux, and Fulford. Well it had been for Harry Morant, born at Bideford, Devon, in 1865, had he come into the world two, or even three centuries earlier, when there was call for bold swash-bucklers, and the Spaniard might always be the honorable prey of a gallant English gentleman seeking to wrest a fortune from Fate with a good right arm. But, unlucky wight, this Devon man was born into the 19th century, with the spirit and temper of the 17th, and, in place of harrying the silver ships of the Dons, with much profit and glory, drifted down to most lowly estate; and, seeking recovery in a new life, died most unhappily. The times were sorrowfully out of joint for him.

As to Harry Morant's parentage, there is truly no need for a chronicler to be too minute of inquiry. If it were possible to search back and name his progenitor in the days when Howard of Effingham was putting out for the Channel—then lined, like a busy street, with the haughty galleons of Spain—that would be well indeed, for from him, whoever he was, Morant took his temper. To some family of note and wealth, it is clear, the boy was born. To what one there is some doubt, his own story not piecing with that of whom he called father. The doubt, I take it, is not one to mourn over. No ancestral vault hungers for the outcast's bones. This much is certainly known, and let it suffice: Harry Morant (that may not have been his real name, but he lived and died with it, making it his own), was Devon born, of gentle family; was given the chance of a good school-learning, but, through being not much given to bookishness, won but little Latin and less Greek; was trained to the English navy and was for some time an officer therein. Throughout a long life in Australia and in South Africa, Harry Morant never departed greatly from his first story as to his birth. It was always Devon which figured in his thoughts- ~the girls of Devon, the horses of Devon, the hounds and foxes of Devon.

That his parents were of some importance many of his friends of the bush and of the camp can testify; and moreover there is the fact that he interrupted his life as a soldier by a visit to Devon, when he hunted with the best of them, and wooed and won to promise of marriage a lady whose sister was betrothed to an officer friend (destined also to meet an unhappy fate with the Bushveldt Carbineers in South Africa).

But little, however, is known as to the facts of the early life of Harry Morant, and that little, coming from his own lips, open to some doubt. The loss, in truth, is not weighty. However these early years were spent, there was little in them, probably, of adventure ; certainly little that would be pleasant to think upon. The man during that time was sinking, sinking down from the level on which he was born, to that of a bush-rover in a land of exile; sinking because his recklessness and rash appetites had put him out of conceit with any honest, settled work or career of sedate usefulness. Probably, not all at once, but after some struggling did Harry Morant succumb to the Erinnyes who pursued him. For, however bleared his eyes in after Australian years, he ever looked backed with longing and regret to a time when his days were young and his life one of promise. In his verses—though they be signed "The Breaker" in full acknowledgment of the writer's station in life as a subduer of wild horses in the wilderness —may be often seen the regret, the longing which thoughts of those in Devon aroused. Herein most particularly—

When other faces turn away,
    And lighter loves have passed;
When life. is weary, cold, and gray—
    I may come back—at last!
When cares, remorse, regrets are rife—
    Too late to live anew—
In the sad twilight of my life
    I will come back—to you!

In his letters, too, many of which are printed in this volume, Morant showed constant thought of Devon. His favorite horse he had named Bideford, in memory of the Devonshire birth-place which he claimed. His familiarity with Devonshire places and people was evident. But what call to argue on the point, or to attempt to lift the veil over those early days in England! It is as bushman and buccaneer that Morant's life came into the light. His past in England may be left buried, if not for his own sake for that of others.

Sometime in the Eighties—even on this point there is some little doubt-Harry Morant drifted to Australia and commenced his career as a bushworker in Queensland. Regarding his life during nearly 20 years as a bushman, no word can be said which will be taken as a reproach among his then peers. If he drank deeply, he rode bravely. If he was fickle to his work, he was true to his mates. He abandoned many a boss, but never a friend.

ENVOI.

*When the last rousing gallop is
  ended.
And the last post-and-rail has been
  jumped.
And a cracked neck that cannot
  be mended
Shall have under the yew-tree
  been "dumped";
Just you leave him alone In God's
  acre—
And drink in wine, whisky or
  beer:
"May the saints up above send
  'The Breaker'
A horse like good old Cavalier,"
  (Signed) His Nibs—*

THE BREAKER.

This is a sketch made by Fred Leist of Harry Morant ("The Breaker"), just before the latter's departure for South Africa. The "Envoi" was written by Morant on the back of the drawing.

Much that helped to make the man an outlaw in Devon helped to make him a hero in the Australian back country, where hard-drinking is no sin, roving recklessness a virtue held in great esteem, and the love of the horse of as good merit as the love of the Lord. His supreme daring, his wonderful horsemanship, his buoyant good humor, his hardy drunkenness—all tended to make Morant a very king in the Australian bush, and the fact that he could break words to his will, as well as horses, and rhyme prettily, added much to his popularity. There is no bush town which Morant visited—and droving in Queensland, N.S. Wales, South Australia, Victoria, he visited very many— that has not to-day sincere mourners for "The Breaker," men ready to swear sturdily that he was no murderer, and to blame anyone but him for those tragedies of the South African veldt which led to his death.

On the banks of the Flinders, the Darling, the Barwon, the Namoi, the Hawkesbury, the Murray, in half a hundred hamlets, Morant at various times lived, and rode and hunted, and mustered, drifting always, when gold was in his pockets, to Sydney, where steeple-chasing, hunting, and the chumship of boon companions of a poetic clan were the lode-stars. On first going to Queensland he took a position as storeman and bookkeeper at a squatter's station—the usual beginning and the usual ending of the derelict "new-chum" who drifts to Australia. But Morant had sterner stuff in him than would be content with adding figures and weighing out tea and sugar. He took to the cattle and the horses, and it was not long before he gave up the dull drudgery of a store-hand, for a drover's life, which promised some outlet for the surging restlessness of his spirit. Failing to find enough to stir him even in that, Morant took to horse-breaking, and subdued many a wild outlaw to the will of man. "He was the only Englishman who could sit a buckjumper like a native" was the sorrowful epitaph of one friend when the death of Morant came to him. That one who rode so well—in hunt and steeplechase, on gallant racer, or wild outlaw——should fall a victim in South Africa, brought home to back-country Australians, perhaps more than all else, the sorrows of war.

There was, in truth, no doubting the splendid courage of Morant. His red recklessness brought him many a broken limb (it was said, with but slight disregard of the truth, that he had been in every country hospital in Australia), but no accident broke his spirit. They tell at Windsor to this day how he rode an unbridled horse bareback at the five-feet fence in front of the local court-house, breaking his own shoulder, and inquiring with his first consciousness as to the well-being of the horse; at Walgett, how he would jump green colts over a four-rail fence ; in another town of his bandaging the eyes of an untried horse to put him at a wire fence. All were useless, feckless deeds, and for that very reason their daring had perhaps a greater charm. Mayhap Morant, in all of them, half hoped for, rather than feared, the end which did not come; and reckless bravery was but the outward sign of a heart timid to shake off the sorrowful burden of life, and hoping to find Death by some happy chance. Perhaps—who knows? Vanity, rather, was the motive, in the thought of one of Morant's mates, who wrote of him,

Harry Morant's deeds of daring were the outcome of the "other man" saying that he "wasn't game." Across the road from the Clarendon racecourse (Hawkesbury), there is an old picket-fence, with a ragged, heart-scaring top. At the hostlery opposite, Morant, after much drinking, wagered Cavalier, the jumping horse, and the one thing he then really loved, to carry him over the picket-fence at a spot reported, on sober word, to be seven feet high. The wager was taken. "The Breaker" put Cavalier at the fence "all out"; the horse swerved but scrambled over.

When the rivers of the back-country were flooded, and the billabongs up, Morant would make his way for miles, enduring much for the sake of an hour's yarn over a bottle of whisky. He and his mate, driving, one time, came to where the backwater from a swollen river had covered the road to the higher country. Only the tops of the wayside fences showed out. But "The

Breaker" decided to go through, and answered a doubt that they might have to turn back: "*I* never turn back."

But of his character and life as an Australian bushman, let his own letters speak. These three were sent to "The Banjo," a friend in the hunting field and the polo course:

Enngonia, Bourke, 3/8/'95.

DEAR PATERSON,—Your letter (*re* Hunt Club races) came along all right, as welcome as a thunderstorm, and set a man yearning for a ride over fences. Would have written you ere this, but a bit of sandal-wood in my right (or should I say " write " ?) hand has made me economical about ink. I have a dingo-skin here, the biggest I have ever seen, and all the local liars say the same of it, which same I will send down to you at the first opportunity. Do for a mat—heads, pads and all attached. Considering the " strychnine and stiffening " character of the country my dingo died a sporting death. The local talent had tried with poison since Christmas last to kill him, but I pulled him down with a couple of cattle-dogs in the moonlight about a Week ago, after a couple or three miles gallop, finishing him with that good old weapon, the stirrup-iron. Killed him within a few hundred yards of a tank-sinker's camp, the pick and shovel men turning" out of their bunks.

> In a mixed kind of costume, half Pontificalibus.
> Half what scholars denominate "Pure naturalibus."

Like Sir Thomas's household in "Ingoldsby."

Filled up some leisure by breaking in a four-year-old colt by the Levite (a Yattendon horse) out of an old mare by The Drummer. The colt was a maneater when I first tackled him, but has turned out a beautiful horse to ride, and I may get a race out of him, as his old mother has won both over hurdles and on the flat.

Like Joseph and John Bunyan of old, " I dreamed a dream "—to the effect that The Admiral had won the Cup, whence came the doggerel you possibly read in " Sporting Notions " a week or so since.

Everything in these parts is devilish dry, and there is small chance of my starting for down the Macquarie with cattle. though I would like to come down and have a ride on Queen Mab. Talking of rhymes, though Lawson's book sold so readily, I fancy his work is very unequal, and, strange to say, his latter jingles and sketches are not all popular with men who have spoken of them to me up here. His best, or, to be correct, his most popular scribbles have appeared over his "Joe Swallow" pen-name, and his identity with that name is, I fancy, mostly unknown. Had an English letter the other day from an old school-fellow, who is at present yachting in the Hebrides to put in the time ere stag-hunting commences in Devon. Stag-hunting starts this week there. How I hate this —— brigalow desert sometimes! Thirty years next Christmas, but feel fifty ! Would like one whole open season, well-carried, in Leicestershire, and wouldn't growl at a broken neck at the finish. A better lot than dreary years in the bush with periodical drunks!

Owing to literally going in bandages, my fist is even more illegible than usual. It would be charitable to finish this scrawl. —Yours in the Brigalow,

HARRY H. MORANT.

This one was dated a little later: —

DEAR PATERSON, —Writing Sydney letters to-day, so send a line. Everything up these parts is dry and dammable. Little grass, less water. Stock poor, and men poorer. If it were to rain shortly I should be able to get down to Sydney, as I have some cattle to shift from an adjacent place to some fellow's paddocks down Warren way.

There are a few scrubbers (cleanskins) yet remaining in an adjoining ten-mile block. The country is fairly dense brigalow and gidgee, and it's not the easiest thing in the world to get them— in fact, we cannot get them, so whenever we want beef here we go out and shoot or "rip"—do you know the latter performance?—and butcher some cheap beef off the beast's hide, Last week my mate and I went beef-hunting. We were riding colts, and had but four revolver cartridges four bullets failed to drop the clean-skin heifer we selected, and I got alongside the heifer to knife her. She turned and charged in her tracks, and the colt, not being up to the game, his bowels came out instead of the heifer's, whilst I was hurled headlong. The colt went off (died that night, poor brute !), and I just managed to put a tree between me and the heifer as she charged. After one or two narrow squeaks—though no beast can catch a man if there is a tree handy—I managed to hamstring her, and the cuddy's misfortune was avenged. Were Frank Mahony about at the time, I guess that illustrations of "Beef-Hunting on the Border" might be worthy of Christmas publication.

I brought a Lancer's spear back with me from Sydney, and find it a first-class weapon for pigs, which are fairly numerous in the lignum of the Culgoa. With a handy horse, pigsticking is not bad fun.

I should like to get down for the Hunt Club Steeple and Point-to-Point, and if rain falls soon I intend to. Trusting that you are all well,—Yours, up country,

HARRY H. MORANT.

———

A Christmas greeting this :—

DEAR PATERSON,—Another Christmas evaporated, thermometer registering something over 110 in the shade each day in the past fortnight. My dislocated shoulder is now as fit as ever. They have an outlawed mare. the Witch, over at Bundaleer station: The boss there gave a fellow a note to ride her twelve months ago. She slung him, and had been spelling since. She was in the yards the other day, and I had a go at her. I have not, as a rule, much respect for sheep-station outlaws, but this one was pretty bad. Up on her hind legs, then backward bucks, and occasionally one or other stirrup banged on the ground. The worst part of her was that one couldn't pull an ounce on her mouth. If you did, the brute would come back with you. I rode her for about an hour, and she was just as bad at the finish as when I got on her, though she would stop when she got the double of a whip round her. I'm not keen on riding her again, anyhow.

In the course of a month or six weeks, I intend departing from these regions to try Coolgardie. If I don't find it prosperous over there, next Christmas will find one prodigal turning up in England with a request for prime veal. —So long,

HARRY H. MORANT.

Finally one giving some hint of his drinking fits :—

DEAR PATERSON,—When I came over here the other day, it was to participate in a hurrah spree to finish the bachelor days of the manager here. He is about to take unto himself a wife of his own ! Most fellows up here generally get shook on, or content with, some other fellow's spouse. Anyhow, I was unsteadily tripping across to my bedroom in the small, murky hours of the morning, and went headlong down some 18ft. of a cellar. Left shoulder dislocated was the result. An amateur surgeon pulled it in again without chloroform next morning, but a ten days complete rest, mostly camping under the flow of an artesian bore, and frequent applications of arnica have put me pretty right once more. I go back to old Morton the end of this week.

Apropos of "The Man from Snowy River," there is a small, sultry border township, ———————— to wit, where, just a year ago, a horse owned by an alleged steward ran a bad second to a shearer's moke, and was declared the winner by the biassed judge.

I have done a bit of brumby running in mountain country, although most of my cleanskin experience has been in mulgoa or brigalow, and I have noticed that a good man on a plucky horse can always beat brumbies when going down a declivity. A horse with a rider on his back goes with confidence, Whilst brumbies are never all out then. When going uphill the naked horse gets away. Weight tells then, I suppose, though, of course, there is the chance of a smash going down.

I must now saddle up for my ride home. With best wishes,—Yours truly,

H. H. MORANT.

———

Many a woman Morant persuaded to love him, quoting to her Herrick and Moore, and Writing for her verses of his own. But the chase and the cup had ever more charm for him than a woman's smile; and he was a listless lover.

So Harry Morant drifted through life, the hope of a return to Devon receding year by year into a dimmer future, steady only in hard drinking and hard riding, seeking forgetfulness in the stupor of one, the excitement of the other, getting quickly older, and shabbier, and nearer to despair, yet his thoughts turning still now and again to England and the possible new life there. In 1899 a big event set his life in a new groove. War began between England and the Boer Republics in South Africa, and the Governments of the Australian States flung themselves into the struggle.

HARRY MORANT-SOLDIER.

TO HARRY MORANT the opening of the gates of the Temple of war was as the opening of prison gates to a captive. He had wearied of life as a bushman. His drinks were becoming a necessity rather than a source of pleasure. The nerve of the man was failing, and there was coming to him the humbling consciousness that that reckless daring, upon which he had more than all else prided himself, depended not solely upon a strong heart, but to some extent upon a healthy liver ; and *that* he no longer had. Before tackling a stiff fence, or a stiff-tempered horse, Morant needed now a "bracer" of brandy or whisky. It is at this stage of a ne'er-do-well's life that he begins to regret and to pine ; to think that existence which is all carouse is not all pleasure, and that a "jug of wine in the wilderness" is not happiness enough after all. When health fails, taste fails, nerve fails, the prodigal yearns for home and domesticity.

In the war between England and the Boers, and in the Australian participation therein, Morant saw a way home, a track to Devon blazed in light. He dreamed of a reputation regenerated in battle, a dead career revivified in glory. Name, fame, home, happiness—these stars shone ahead, through the smoke of desperate struggles, in which Harry Morant, sword in hand, moved as Mars incarnate, invincible by his daring and prowess. To his friends Morant confided these dear hopes, and set about entering upon his career as a soldier, with more of fixed purpose than his futile life had yet shown. He had an influential relative at Adelaide, South Australia. So it was at that capital that he chose to enlist. To have applied for a commission would have been hopeless : the dare-devil, hard-drinking roysterer knew that, but the future held for him as much and more. To be plain "Trooper Morant " was only the beginning: the rest would follow in due course: as a soldier he saw a "way out " —out of the hard, exacting toil of the bush, out of the ingrained habit of "knocking-down" a cheque so soon as earned. Baptised in the fire of battle he would enter upon a new life.

Morant's conduct when he joined the South Australian Mounted Rifles (second contingent) was at the outset exemplary. Almost at once he was made a corporal, and in a short while rose to the rank of sergeant. Getting to the front, he was, with most of the mounted Australians, attached to General French's cavalry column, on which fell the brunt of Lord Roberts famous advance, that outflanked Cronje at Magersfontein, relieved Kimberley, destroyed a Boer army at Paardeberg, and captured Bloemfontein. But there is reason to believe that Morant was very quickly disillusioned as to the nature of a war career. The opportunities were not so good, his resolution was not so strong, as he had imagined. " Turning over a new leaf," under the stimulus of frequent battles and quick promotion, he had looked on as an easy task; and it might have proved so. But in this campaign there were few battles ; but much hard riding ; and much ill-treatment of good horses, which "savaged " him; and much cattle-thieving, which corrupted him. He soon found that there was very little call for a regenerated Harry Morant, moving through the thick ranks of an enemy with flashing sword and kindling eye ; but there was very real need for the old Harry Morant, daring rider, reckless adventurer, sadly confused in mind as to the ethics of horse acquisition. And the man there was need for came to the surface. Devon was still thought of : " Home " was still the object. But Fate, unhappily, made the path much easier to his feet than he had thought. It was not, however, an upward path.

Morant's bold riding first attracted the attention of General French, who made him a despatch-rider. Then Mr. Bennett Burleigh, the war correspondent of the London

DAILY TELEGRAPH, was struck by this fine horseman and not indifferent writer, and Morant left his regiment to assist that gentleman in some capacity or another. He still was horse-stealer and mule-snarer-in-chief to headquarters staff, however, and his services to the Remount Department in bringing in animals were acknowledged by several presents. On the whole, Morant had an easy, pleasant life, and withal, made money. He accompanied General French's column through the Carolina and Barberton districts, under no particular bonds of discipline, in a position which was somewhat literary and somewhat horsey- a position entirely suitable to his temperament, but little suitable to those ideas of regeneration with which he had left Australia.

The prime object of his campaigning Morant, however, still kept in view, and in a moment of weariness, having the means at hand in the shape of a good supply of cash, he threw up the business— soldiering, war-corresponding, horse-stealing, and what not, and sped to Devon. True he had not won his commission ; a V.C. and a D.S.O. were still lacking. But he had been following, for a full year, what in England would be regarded as a respectable and indeed honorable calling. His pockets were well-lined, and Harry Morant stepped ashore at Plymouth, reasonably elate. The days of horse-breaking, droving, and of bush sprees were done with, and he was on the path back to his heritage. For some three months the soldier lived a gallant life in Devon--hunting, love-making, banquetting. He chased the fox, following the hounds of Mark Rolle-descendant of that famous Devonshire gentleman who, at Haldon Hall, on July 23rd, 1690, with 500 others assembled, without summons, without call, to push French Admiral Tourville back to the sea. He engaged himself to a Devon lass, and seems to have established fairly amicable relations with his "people." Then either his money or his welcome, or his fondness for a peaceful, if not quiet life, exhausted —Morant bethought again of the war. There was still call for men, though Lord Roberts had announced the end of the struggle, and his application for a post was promptly granted. Morant had on this occasion a better startingpoint. He

figured, not as a drover whose sprees were the talk of a conti-
nent, but as Devonshire gentleman, who had already done me-
ritorious service as a volunteer. So Harry Morant went back to
South Africa as a conimissioned officer in Baden-Powell's constabulary, entitled to draw generous pay and to wear a uniform,
whose great gorgeousness was to its ingenious designer matter for trouble afterwards. But Morant never took up his duties
with the constabulary. Possibly a mere restlessness of disposi-
tion, possibly a thought that there was better promise in another quarter, changed the man's intentions; and on landing in
Capetown, he applied to Colonel Mackay, stationed there with
the duty of administering any business in connection with the
Australian troops, for employment in some military capacity.
Colonel Mackay remembered that Major R. Lenehan was then
forming a regiment, to be know as the Bushveldt Carbineers,
for service as a body of Irregular Horse in the Northern Transvaal, and sent Morant on to him. "The Bushveldt Carbineers"!
("Bushveldt Buccaneers," as the Australian BULLETIN christe-
ned them aptly, too, to the original meaning of the term, when
it was first applied to the reckless, filibustering French hunters
in America.) Of that ill-fated corps, so closely associated with
the later history of Harry Morant, a word must be said here.

"The Bushveldt Carbineers " never actually existed as a regiment. It was proposed to form such a corps; recruiting was
undertaken, volunteers were enrolled ; but the regiment was never really formed : what there was of the body, at the time of the
arrest of its officers, was abruptly disbanded. Early in 1900, soon
after Lord Kitchener had taken command in South Africa, a proposal was made by a Jewish storekeeper* named Levy, living at

---

* A curious circumstance of recent South African history is the mutual hatred
between the Boers and the Jews, who might be imagined to have had a bond of
union in their common admiration of the Old Testament. It is related of Pre-
sident Kruger that, having consented to open a synagogue, built by the Jews of
Johannesburg, he took that occasion to flout their faith by declaring it open "in
the name of the Lord Jesus Christ."

the Pienaars River, that "the loyal British subjects " of the Pieters-burg district (Northern. Transvaal) should be organised into a regiment to subjugate that stretch of country. At this time no British troops had penetrated further than Warm Baths. Beyond that town, though a railway ran to Pietersburg, the country was in the undisputed possession of the Boers. Mr. Levy backed up his recommendation by a cash offer of £1000 towards the organisation of the corps, and it was decided to fall in with his idea. Major Lenehan, a N.S.W officer, who had served with some distinction on General Anderson's staff in the East, Where he had commanded a column of mounted infantry in the Machadodorp district, was asked to organise the new regiment and take its command. He agreed. It was very soon found that Mr. Levy's estimate of the numerical strength of the "loyal British subjects" in the Pietersburg district was not at all correct; only 30 such volunteers came forward. Major Lenehan reported this to Lord Kitchener, and suggested that, if the proposal to form the regiment were persisted in, its strength could best be made up by recruiting time-expired Australian soldiers. The suggestion was adopted, and it was decided to offer the inducement of seven shillings a day (which was two shillings a day in excess of the ruling Colonial rate) to recruits. Tempted by this, volunteers began to drift in.

It seems to have been pretty generally understood from the first that the Bushveldt Carbineers were to undertake a different class of work to that of the general army. Exactly what the instructions given to its officers were it is, of course, impossible to know with the exactness of truth. At the court-martial on the officers of the Carbineers it was sworn by the accused, and by one other witness, that they had orders "not to take any prisoners." Whence these orders emanated, whether indeed they were given at all by anyone in authority, it is not my intention to discuss here at any length. What is merely rumor-either with regard to the crimes of the Carbineers or their justification—falls outside the province of this book. This much may be set forth as certain: that among the officers of the Bushveldt Carbineers there was a general thought that the strong arm was not to be restrained by the merciful heart. The war against the Boers had now entered upon a stage when some degree of exasperation was inevitable on either side -on the one because resistance was being prolonged beyond the point at which it seemed reasonable; on the other because with grim certainty of failure there had come but a strengthening of the belief that resistance was a holy duty. The British forces were now under a new General, whose name was associated in the army's camp-talk with all that was severe and stern in time of war. The Bushveldt Carbineers were sent to the front without any of the hampering restrictions which tied the hands of the regulars. They were paid special rates as a body of "Irregular" Horse. All these circumstances seemed to them to point to the conclusion that sterner work was plotted out for them than the patrol duties of regular cavalry. Whatever their orders, then, from headquarters, the Carbineers considered, with perhaps good reason, that theirs was a special mission of destruction.

HARRY MORANT
From a Photograph taken in 1886.

The first invitations for volunteers for the Bushveltd Carbineers, in spite of the big pay offered, were not responded to eagerly: the full strength of the regiment was never reached. But a few companies were in time got together, and they acted as scouts in front of General Plumer's advance to Pietersburg.

From the beginning their collisions with the Boers were stern. To prevent the British forces using the railway line to aid their advance was the chief object of the Boer tactics: trains, and the permanent way itself, were therefore constantly destroyed by dynamite. The Carbineers, on whom, as scouts, the brunt of the fighting fell, finally adopted the plan of collecting Boers from the country side and sending them along the railway line on a truck before the pilot engine. Two or three times the forced hostages were blown up by dynamite. It is on record that an English officer objected to these tactics at first, as being against the rules of war. But, against the rules or not, in spite of protests, the Boers were used in this way, and hoist by, their countrymen's petards, to the great satisfaction of the scouting Carbineers. Sullenly, savagely the Boers fell back, abandoning train-wrecking as a means of defence. In due course the British force reached Pietersburg, and established a fort there. The war in the district had commenced with evil omens of cruelty and undisciplined hatred Such inauspicious beginning had been made, when in April, 1901, Harry Morant entered the office of Major Lenehan, recruiting officer for the Bushveldt Carbineers, saluted and asked for employment, producing a recommending letter from Colonel Mackay. It was a different Morant to the man with whom Major Lenehan had been familiar in Australia-a trim, well-dressed, well-set-up fellow bearing himself with none of the reckless air of old. Possibly the Major recalled the time, not so long before, when Morant had ridden in the Amateur Steeplechase at Randwick, Sydney, on Colonel Airey's Bay Lady, had had a fall, but, that despite, had attended at a dinner and theatre party the same evening—in a dress suit obviously belonging to some smaller man. There was no trace of that careless roysterer in the Morant of 1901, attired in the ultra-baggy riding breeches of an English "masher," speaking with the easy confidence of the man who is getting on in the world. Major Lenehan at once agreed to give Morant a lieutenancy, and sent him up to Pietersburg with the next batch of recruits. Before leaving Pretoria, however, Harry Morant stayed a few days with Captain Hunt, also a Bushveldt Carbineer and an old acquaintance. The two officers were engaged to marry sisters in England: they were of the same habits, and had many other bonds of union. With him Morant went to the front to begin his career as a buccaneer.

HARRY MORANT -BUCCANEER.

TRULY, what had been promised in the beginning was being accomplished in the Pietersburg district. As the twig was bent, the tree grew; and those first days of sullen resentment— of outrage rather than of war—had tinged the whole course of the campaign in the Bushveldt country. It was Morant's unhappy Fate that he should have been sent to the one place where most of all was needed a cool head, a stern judgment, and a wise heart——of which none he had—to avoid dark disgrace.

The first task assigned to Lieutenant Morant was the guardianship of the Chunesport and Strydeport Passes, two defiles beyond Pietersburg. That town was now strongly garrisoned, but the out-district was still subject to sudden forays by Boer commandoes, that at times threatened the fortress itself. The passes of which Morant had the guardianship were of some strategical worth in the defence of the town. But he did not content himself with merely keeping the enemy at a distance. By frequent raids into Boer territory he harried the Dutch population, gathering in many prisoners and cattle. No charge of inhumanity was alleged against Morant in connection with these expeditions. Life was to him then very pleasant—plenty of fighting, and yet not all fighting, for frequently he was able to get away from his post at Strydeport to Pietersburg to play polo or dine and yarn with the officers of the British garrison. The gay-hearted Australian, dare-devil rider, expert polo-player, witty talker, was in great favor those days, and Fortune seemed indeed to smile upon him.

In June the Bushveldt Carbineers pushed forward their outposts. Captain Taylor, a political agent, said to be deep in the confidence of the chief authorities, had arrived at Pietersburg, and had drawn 50 men from the " regiment " and taken them

North. With Captain Taylor, who held no military command, went Lieutenant Handcock, a N.S.W. officer, afterwards shot with Morant. Meanwhile, with the passing of time, warfare between the British and Boers in this district had become yet more savage. It was stated by the Boers that the English were "stirring up " the Kaffirs, had secret agents in the district for that purpose : on the other side was the bitter resentment caused by a renewal of train-wrecking, and consequent fatalities on the railways. Later in June a second detachment of Bushveldt Carbineers was taken out from Pietersburg to Spelonken-50 men under Captain Hunt, with Lieutenant Morant as second in command. Coming to a Kaffir kraal some 70 miles from Pietersburg this party added to its defences, and constructed Fort Edward. The time was now approaching for those tragedies with which the name of the Bushveldt Carbineers* will be for ever linked.

Before entering upon the story of these dark happenings—a word as to the varied stories regarding the Carbineers which have obtained currency, both in Australia and England. The officers of the ill-fated corps have been, by divers accounts, represented as fiends incarnate, drunken murderers and robbers, killing Boers for the sake of their gold, and mercilessly sacrificing women and children to their thirst for blood. Let it in fairness be said that all this is mere allegation, much of it obviously false. That the Carbineers cruelly broke the rules of war is certain; that more murders were committed by them than those sheeted home may be surmised without injustice. But let it be remembered that, after it had been charged against them that they had killed a German subject, the actions of the corps were scrupulously scrutineered by a British Commission of Inquiry

---

* So that he may better understand the movements of the Bushveldt Carbineers the reader is advised to study the map printed on page 42—a "Service map" roughly drawn, but giving all essential distances.

Chunesport Pass-Morant's First Post.

which, though it might have been sympathetic to men who had gone beyond the mark in Boer-killing, was probably on the whole just, and showed a very clear resolution to get to the bottom of things. If it had been possible for that Court of Inquiry to have brought before the subsequent court-martial charges of drunken atrocities, and of shooting prisoners for the sake of their money, assuredly it would have done so, as likely to attract sympathy to the accusers, and to take from them some of the odium attaching to the punishment of the offenders. But no such allegations were made. The official record of the charges on which the officers were found guilty reads :—

(1) H. H. Morant, P. J. Handcock, G. R. Witton and H. Picton, of the Bushveldt Carbineers, were charged with —
Charge: When on active service, committing the offence of murder, August 11, (one victim).

Finding: The court find the prisoner Morant guilty of murder, but find the prisoners Handcock, Witton and Picton guilty of manslaughter.

(2) H.H. Morant, P.J. Handcock and G.R. Witton, of the Bush veldt Carbineers, were charged with-
Charge: When on active service committing the offence of murder, August 23, 1901 (eight victims).
Finding : The court find the prisoners guilty of the charge.

(3) H.H. Morant and P. J. Handcock, of the Bushveldt Carbineers, were charged with —
Charge: When on active service, committing the offence of murder, September 7th, 1901 (three victims).

Finding : The court find the prisoners guilty of the charge.
Sentence: The court sentences the prisoners Morant, Handcock and Witton to suffer death by being shot, and the prisoner Picton to be cashiered.

A Group of Bushveldt Carbineers. (The man in the center is holding a wart-hog).

(4)Major R. W. Lenehan, Bushveldt Carbineers, was charged with—Charge:
When on active service, by culpable neglect, omitting to make a report
   which it was his duty to make.
Finding 2 The court find the prisoner guilty of the charge.
Sentence : The court sentences the prisoner to be reprimanded.
The finding and sentences have been confirmed by the General
   Commanding in chief.

There was one other allegation and one other trial, when Handcock was charged with having at or near Bandolier Kop, in the Transvaal, on the 23rd August, 1901, wilfully murdered one C. A. D. Hesse, a German missionary. Morant was charged with having instigated and commanded Handcock to commit the murder. On this charge both prisoners were found not guilty.

That these 12 victims, the murder of whom was sheeted home, made up the total unfairly sent to death by the Bushveldt Carbineers is not reasonably believable. It is probable that many more were killed quietly, and no word heard. It was on the whole a "no-quarter" warfare , Which was being waged in the outer Pietersburg district. At the court-martial on Morant he swore that he had, from the first, distinct orders from Captain Hunt not to bring in prisoners, and that he understood these orders were from head-quarters: and another Witness gave evidence that he had heard Captain Hunt reprimand Lieutenant Morant for bringing in prisoners. On the numerous forays of the Carbineers and of other troops in the neighbourhood, then, it may be taken for a fact, that many Boers were killed outside the exigencies of actual warfare. And it may be accepted also on the other side, as a fact, that the stories which give a squalid object to the murders, and surround them with circumstances of most savage atrocity and drunken revelling, are fictitious. The Bushveldt Carbineers played the part of remorseless guerillas. The shame of that they must bear. It is enough without adding imaginative horrors.

On July 3rd, 1901, Captain Hunt with 12 others left Fort Edward in pursuit of Viljoen. Following them south through the Madjadjes hills (where reigned the prototype of Rider Haggard's

"She," a Kaffir princess who lived to an extraordinary age), past Reuter's (German) mission station, the Carbineers came upon the Boers at Devil's Kloof. There opened a series of grim, dark tragedies, when those 13 men on the morning of Saturday, July 6, advanced to the attack of the ominously named farm. The house was well held by the Boers, and the storming party beaten back, leaving Captain Hunt—dead or wounded—on the field. According to one account the captain was wounded only, and afterwards was foully murdered in cold blood by the Boers: another story states that he was killed in action, but his body was afterwards mutilated: yet another one that he was in no wise despitefully treated, either living or dead, by his enemies. Of these things no man may speak certainly : but at the time and on the spot the Carbineers believed the worst of the Boers. Nor indeed, such was the most unhappy cruelty of the war in the district, was it difficult to believe that— or aught else cruel and unnatural.

When the news was brought to Harry Morant his rage was terrible. He wept for the dead, and raved against the living. Captain Hunt had been his dear brother-in-arms, and was to be his brother in marriage : was best of chums at table, in the polo field, and in the clash of battle. It was not a fair chance of war that he should have thus fallen. And the men who had been with him? Cowards, cowards, cowards, to leave him, wounded or dead, in the hands of the enemy ! Morant in rage and grief called the garrison together to address them, but broke down utterly, to incoherent weeping and vague cursing. It was another officer who took his place and spoke to the troops, urging them to avenge their captain's loss. With grim hearts the men rode out from Fort Edward, Lieutenant Morant leading them, sternly set upon avenging the blood of a comrade and wiping out from their own names the stain of cowardice. When men move in a such mood it is ill for those who chance to meet them.

The Bushveldt Carbineers, urged on by Morant (who from

this day for many days after was no longer a gay, light-hearted man, but stern and sullen, the death of his friend seeming to eat into his heart) pushed on with great speed, and having left Fort Edward on the 7th August, did actually reach Reuter's mission station, a good 85 miles distant, by the next day. There lived Herr Reuter, a German preacher, and there Morant heard from the lips of Aaron, who was Kaffir servant to Captain Hunt, how the captain had been wounded, then most brutally murdered and stripped. The body was there, sorrily mangled in truth—whether in loathsome spite or in sad but unavoidable happening of battle no man can say with certainty. But Morant, hearing, in no particular disbelieved Aaron's story ; and his heart grew more savage, and his face took a sterner set as he saddled up again and followed on the track of the Boers. Not war but vengeance was in his mind.

The men of Vilojen´s troop, however, avoided dark death on this occasion. Morant, always eagerly pushing on, ceaselessly conferring with his officers, telling them that up to this he had refused to carry out orders and shoot prisoners taken, but henceforth there was to be no mercy, came up with the enemy on August 9th, at Reitvlei. The Boers were in laager, and Morant disposed of his 80 men in three troops, intending to surround them. But the enemy were in their own country, and knew it well. The attackers found that impenetrable swamps protected the laager on two sides, and in these swamps Morant, who was leading the centre, became entangled whilst yet 1,500 yards from the Boers. Eager as he was, Morant opened fire from there. The Boers in alarm rushed from their laager, leaving all they possessed behind them, but saving their lives.

A Fort used by the Bushveldt Carbineers.

Nay, not all of them. Getting to the camp the Carbineers found one sick man, Visser his name, in a waggon. Visser was wounded and had not been able to join in the rush from the camp. He was found wrapped in a cloak which had belonged to Captain Hunt. This one victim was carried along with the Carbineers, whose leader still brooded over the loss of his friend ; and next morning a " drum-head court-martial " was instituted, and Visser condemned to death. The sick man was taken from his waggon and shot, and the Carbineers rode home with the first (so far as is certainly known) stains of blood, taken in guilt, upon their hands. Perhaps to some of them the mock tribunal, called a "drum-head court-martial," gave color of lawfulness to this murder, but murder it was and naught else.

It was not possible for Morant, strongly -though he wished it, to follow on the trail of the fleeing commando. He had practically stripped Fort Edward of its garrison, and in that Fort were the stores and supplies on which the little band depended for their very existence. So faces were turned homewards and moodily the troop rode back, their thirst for blood not assuaged by the sacrifice of Visser.

Of Lieutenant Morant's feelings at this time there are clear indications in his correspondence. This letter was written very shortly after the return of the troop to Fort Edward (it makes no mention, it will be noted, of Visser's death, and the silence on that point suggests that the writer had some idea of the darkness of the deed.)

Saturday Morning, 17/8/01, Spelonken.
MY DEAR MAJOR,—A runner goes to Pietersburg this morning, so just a hasty note, as I happen to be in camp. You will know how cut up we must have been over poor old Hunt's death. I'll never get such a good pal as he proved himself to be. I wish to the Lord that I'd been out with him that night,—he might have got wiped out all the same; but the d—d Dutchmen who did it would never have left the house. We've killed 13 of them up to date, now—and that crowd haven't a blanket left to wrap themselves in. It was a
d———d hard job to write to Hunt's girl, which same I did after we returned. Poor old Hunt! God rest his soul! but he "died decent." I've lost my best

mate, and you've lost your best officer.

We're getting along very well up here. Whips o'work. News comes in every day of small parties of Boers; and out we go to harry 'em like b———cattle dogs. We've given this quarter a pretty hot name for the Boers, and they all are drifting to the WATERBERG; gathering up there to some considerable number by this time. We're whipping them in; "getting them together "; and IT WANTS A STRONG FORCE -a column—to smash them once they get consolidated there. One great requirement here is HORSE SHOES. For the Lord's sake send up *half-a-dozen boxes* at least. We've got the shoes literally worn off the horses' hoofs—with work I make men out on patrol walk and lead at every opportunity ; and considering the work done the horses last out and look well. The Sergt. -Major (Hammet) you sent up is an excellent man; has a big grip of the men ; knows his work, and makes the men do theirs! With the men getting 7/- per day; they ought to be pretty freely "culled," and get a better quality of soldier without damaging the numbers to any extent! By G———, there must have been some wastrels there that night when poor old Hunt went under. I suppose Mortimer has told you that his body was stripped, neck broken, etc., etc., by the Boers. I've straightened some of them up. They stand cursing ! But you cannot make crooked stick straight, or make a d———d coward a good plucked one. I fancy you've heard some fairy tales to the detriment of Taylor ! You must remember the source they come from. Hunt got on with him famously right from the first, and I, Hancock, and the rest of us couldn't wish for a better fellow to work with. We work ourselves, men and horses d———d hard, but Taylor lends us every assistance, and his "intelligence " is the most reliable I've struck in South Africa. Hancock you know ! and I find him worth the other two in himself. You must excuse my apparent carelessness in the matter of letter writing, but I have really not had any chance of scribbling. If ever I sat down to write, some d———d Boers bobbed up and we had to go out and " worry " them. By the way, if there are any scattered things of Hunt's about Pietersburg camp, will you look after them *personally* ? Poor old chap—he left his ponies and all his gear to me, and I've got something to fix up for him, which, as it's a very private matter, I will not write of : but will inform you privately as our C.O. when I see you. If you could only come up here for a week, I think it would do a power of good in many ways, and I hope, if you do come up, you will not be dissatisfied with our work.—Good-bye, Major !—Yours obediently, _

HARRY H. MORANT. "Tony."

And later, whilst in Pietersburg gaol, Morant in the last letter, so far as is known, written by him, attempted to justify his actions:

MY DEAR MAJOR,——Hell to pay ! Isn't it ?—(*you* are all right and will live to go hunting again). If anything happens to me you write to my governor: and to my girl (————, N. Devon). Also see *Bulletin* people in Sydney town and tell 'em all the facts. How Hunt was shot by Boers, and how I "carried on " same as he would have done—had *I* been shot that night at Viljoen's. Had I tumbled into Boer hands, I'd have gone on whilst I had a cartridge left, and then used the butt, and then have been *wiped out*. That's what I'd expect if I had fallen into Boer lines—wouldn't have "groused" either—it would have been just part of the programme—War ! But it is damned rough this treatment ! from our own British (?) side !

However, I put my faith in the Lord and Headquarters, Pretoria, and hope to see a fox killed and kiss a Devon girl, again.

Buck-up, old man. Had I known as much two months ago as I know to-day —there would be a lot of Dutchmen at large that are now in Hell, or the Bermudas.

I've starved and trekked, and done my work tolerably successfully — from the Buck River to the Portuguese Border—and the result is :

D.	S.	O.
a	i	f
m	l	f
n	ly	i
		c
		er

Hope we go home together, *if not*
          Write to
            My Guvnor
            Girl
            and *Bulletin.*
     Thine,

                   TONY LUMPKIN.

Bushveldt Carbineers on horse - Major Lenehan in Command.

The second atrocity of which Morant was guilty occurred on the night of August 23rd. A patrol of Bushveldt Carbineers, by native runner, reported to Fort Edward that eight Boer surrenderers were being brought in. Lieutenant Morant took out with him Lieutenants Handcock and Witton and three men, and went to meet the convoy. Taking the Boers from their waggons he had them shot at once in cold blood, without even pretence of trial.

The signal of death given by Morant Was: "That's for Captain Hunt."

The third murders followed quickly on, and were marked by the same deliberate cruelty. On August 7th three Boer prisoners— two men and a boy—were taken from a patrol by Lieutenants Morant and Handcock, and summarily shot.

The blood-tale was now complete, so far as proved outrages were concerned. There is strong reason, unhappily, to believe that other murders are entered against officers of the Bushveldt Carbineers in those Records from which human uncertainty is absent, and the whole truth is set down of all this world's happenings. A German missionary named Hesse, who had learned something of the doings of the Carbineers, set out for Pietersburg to protest to the authorities there. He was shot on the way—by whom it is not possible to say with certainty, but not difficult to guess. A trooper of the Carbineers was also, it is said by some, shot : he was in the same plight as Hesse, a protester against outrages, and died in the same fashion. But in time news trickled through to Pietersburg of the happenings of August and September. Not all the people who carried ugly facts died providentially on the way, and the British authorities learned of a series of murders of which there could be no apparent palliation. There is strong reason to believe also that, almost at the same time, the German Government was apprised. There were several German subjects in the district, and one of them had been among the supposed victims. Major Lenehan, the officer commanding the Bushveldt Carbineers, who had so far seen no active service with the corps, was sent up to take charge at Fort Edward, to inquire into the truth of the charges, and to put an end to any lawlessness.

Major Lenehan found Morant a changed man—morose, irritable, gloomy: thought indeed that he saw symytoms of mental weakness in him, and had some notions of relieving the lieutenant of his command. At the time, it happened that there was a fresh irruption of Boer commandoes into the Pietersburg district, and the position at Fort Edward was somewhat anxious. Commandant Tom Kelly, an Irishman, a splendid fighter, and one of the most hated of the Boer irregular leaders, was threatening on one side: and Commander Beyers, with a big body of Boers, on another. It was of pressing importance that Tom Kelly should be captured. This Morant impressed upon Lenehan, who was also well aware of the fact. But the commander hesitated about sending his subordinate out on the trail. The lieutenant prayed for the chance.

" But," objected the senior officer, " we particularly want this man brought in alive."

"Alive?" interjected Morant. "Don't you know what a b——— scoundrel he is ?"

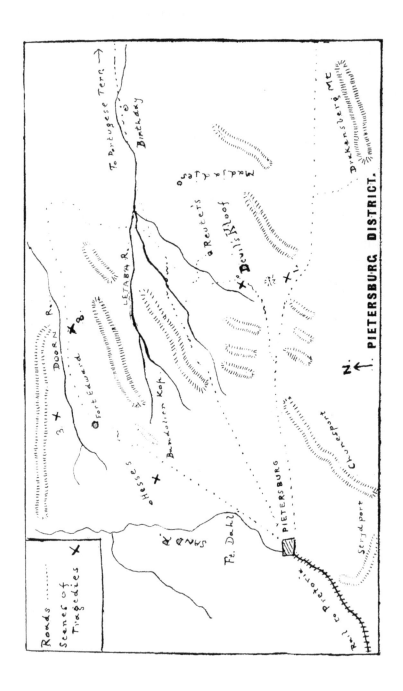

Finally Morant was allowed to take a patrol out after Tom Kelly. But he knew that Kelly, if captured, was not even to be allowed to commit suicide, or meet with a fatal accident: else there would be awkward need of explanation. The pursuit and capture of Commander Kelly was the last soldierly duty that fell to the lot of Morant, and right well he carried it out. Pursuing Kelly with an almost equal force, right to the edge of the Portuguese border, he captured him and his commando in the very teeth of a small "army," with which Commander Beyers tried to intercept him.

This was Morant's despatch, written on the field, recording the capture:

25/9/01,
25 Miles E, by S. of the Birthday Mine.

To O.C. B.V.C., Pietersburg.

SIR,—I have the honor to report the capture of the Boer Veldt Cornet Tom Kelly and nine (9) other Boers. On the evening of the 22nd, Sunday, I dismounted my patrol at BANNIELLA's (Kaffir) Kraal, and laagered the horses. At 8.30 I proceeded in the reported direction of Kelly's Laager with the patrol on

Morant at the head of his Company (Fort Edward).

foot. At 10.20 p.m. I arrived in the near vicinity of the Boer camp. Halting the men, I made a personal reconnoissance of the laager with CONSTAN-TEON, of the Intelligence Department, and found out the exact situation of waggons and surroundings. As there were Women in the camp I refrained from shooting. I divided the patrol into three troops of 10 men. Leaving one with Sergt.-Hammet at 150 yards from the Boer camp, I took the other with Lieut. Witton into the river bed, which ran under a steep bank around Kelly's waggons. There we lay quietly until 4.30 a.m., Monday 23rd instant, when we charged the camp with rifles loaded. The camp was taken completely at a surprise. I took Kelly´s rifle whilst he was still in bed, and the camp put their hands up sulkily as the B.V.C collected their rifles, etc. This occurred on the Thsombo River, a short 12 miles from the Portuguese Border, and 130 miles from Fort Edward, our camp at the Spelonken. Kelly had, but a few days prior to his capture, refused to surrender to the Portuguese authorities, and threatened to give any English " a warm reception " if they came after him. His rifles, with the exception of one Mauser, and his saddle gear, are all British, which his people have captured early in the war, I will give further details upon my arrival at Fort Edward. I hope to be back in camp on Tuesday next, the 1st October. Kelly and the nine Boers are the last remnant of a commando which has caused much trouble in the Spelonken district, and his capture rendered this district free from the enemy. Men and horses of the patrol are all well, though the horses are only grass fed (no mealies), and the troops living till we reach the Birthday Mine on what game the country affords. Kelly's crowd are intact, and I trust to give a safe delivery. As the country is now clear, I should like permission to escort these prisoners personally to Pietersburg, leaving Lieut. Hancock in charge of the fort, as if possible I would like very much to go to Pretoria for at couple of days to settle up the affairs of my friend, the late Captain Hunt, as he wished me to. I will write you upon my arrival at Spelonken.—I have the honor to be, Sir, yours obediently,

HARRY MORANT, Lieutenent.

O.C. B.V.C., Spelonken.

Morant was granted the fortnight's leave for which he applied, went to Pretoria, and returned to Pietersburg—to be arrested on charges of murder. The other officers of the Bushveldt Carbineers were also put under arrest on various charges, and the corps disbanded. Morant was kept in close solitary confinement during the inquiry into the charges against him.

HARRY MORANT'S
IMPRISONMENT-AND RELEASE

—

THE Court of Inquiry into the allegations of murder against the Bushveldt Carbineers began its sittings in October, 1901. The officers of the Carbineers were, from the opening of the sessions, held as close prisoners, special precautions being taken against allowing any communication between them. Still some words passed, and Morant's gaol letters are not the least interesting of his writings. This, one of the earliest, gives a hint of the close inquiry that was being made into the records of the Bushveldt Carbineers. It is undated :

The C. Commandant wanted to know what I knew about a jackal-skin kuross, which Hunt obtained from one Majoto—a notorious Kaffir scoundrel who alleged that he had not been paid for it. I replied in writing to the effect that I *knew* (as did the mess corporal) that Hunt had purchased and paid for (in legal S. A. tender) the same kuross, and had given it to you. It appears that this d——d Hottentot (Majoto) is trying to get it back to give it to—?—?! When a C.C. pals with a Kaffir of questionable character, and that person's word is taken alongside that of a British officer, some folk are playing all they know, and a bit low down at that. Have worn breeches twice, so am getting them washed before sending them along. The Governor (my dad) got a K.C.B. the other day in " birthday honors." Hunt's affairs were settled up satisfactorily yesterday. The C.O. of P.L.H. is obviously a decent chap—treated me as such, too—in marked difference to alleged officers and gentlemen (save the mark !) of a line regiment in indifferent odour. God Save Oireland and ship me home quick ! If we only can see a fox killed this season.—Thine, despondently,

                                                          "TONY."

Other letters written from the Pietersburg gaol, sometimes only from one cell to another, show the grim humor with which the prisoner took his confinement. In a spirit of jest the notes were headed as from Dartmoor, Darlinghurst, Pentridge and other well-known gaols. Here are two (inserted not quite in the chronological order of happenings) :

Dartmoor!

DEAR HANNAM,—Send you herewith some books—though they're mostly "Tripe!" I'm getting fat—showing *"emponbong"* owing to confinement! Hell ! No more hunting ! No more partridges ! No trimset petticoat !

All on account of the unity of the Empire!! Should the Lord allow that I ever see Ushant Light 4 points on the starboard bow, once more, and steam safe into Southampton waters or Plymouth Sound, the only *Empire* I'll acknowledge is where—

At 7.45 they open the doors
And the Promenade's flooded with London's ——s
God Save Oireland !—Thine,

TONY.

Lieut. Hannam, per favor Gar, -Adjt.

Darlinghurst! ! 11/12/01.

DEAR MAJOR,—I received from a Captain Bell a memo about my horse "Bideford Boy" being on the Pietersburg Light Horse lines. Do you remember a *black* that Hunt left in charge of Anderson V.O. when we first navigated towards Spelonken? The black, which was a private horse of Hunt's, was a very fair polo nag, and that is why he did not take it on trek with us. I have an idea that the horse was returned to B.V.C. lines, and that Neel had care of it. I should like to find out what has become of it. Everything of mine and Hunt's in Pretoria. had been looted from our house. I blame Johnson for d——d carelessness; even fox marks and brushes were taken! Talking of marks and brushes !—this is December—they're killing foxes down in Devon with Mark Rolle's hounds, whilst I am "helping to save the Empire," in d——d D——d solitary confinement. Of such is the Kingdom of Brass Hats! Can you tell me what became of the black ? as I wish to get the nag before a Government brand is applied—if that has been done some-one will have to compensate. I haven't written home or to Hunt's people since I've been knee-haltered.—Thine,

"TONY."

Please answer : or who would know what became of that horse?

HANDCOCK. MORANT. DR. JOHNSON. HUNT. TAYLOR. PICTON.

Group of Bushveldt Carbineer Officers and others.

Another characteristic letter was printed in the last chapter :
and a set of verses penned in gaol is reproduced in this volume. Throughout there is shown no very serious forebo-
ding of the future. It evidently did not even come to the
mind of Morant that a capital penalty might be exacted for
his misdeeds. Probably the utmost that he feared was de-
gradation from his rank—the final and irretrievable ruin of
that hope of his of regeneration through a soldier's career.
The Court of Inquiry conducted its deliberations in strict
secrecy, and made none of its findings public. But, as a result of
those findings, a series of court-martials opened on January 21st.
The decisions ultimately arrived at were that Major Lenehan was
guilty of failure to report one of the incidents, and was reprimanded: that Lieutenant Morant was guilty of 12 murders on
three separate dates, and was sentenced to be shot: and that
Lieutenants Handcock, Witton and Picton were guilty either
of participation in, or complicity with, some of these murders.
(Handcock was shot. Witton sentenced to imprisonment for
life. Picton cashiered). The accused persons were represented
by counsel (Major J. F. Thomas, an Australian), and seem to
have had on the whole a fair trial.

The course of justice was destined to be disturbed most
dramatically. When the Bushveldt Carbineers were disbanded,
the formation was attempted of a body to be known as the Pietersburg Light Horse, to take up the "irregular" work where it
had been stopped. But recruiting for the Light Horse was not
very successful, and raiding against the Boers was practically
put a stop to, for lack of raiders. The Carbineers had followed
the plan of throwing themselves out into the country, many miles distant from headquarters, leaving behind no settled lines
of communication, trusting to their rifles for both safety and
food. They, in fact, played a guerilla game against the Boers, and
very marked was the success of their stern forays in keeping the
Boer power from coming to a head in the district. De Wet himself was no greater thorn in the side of an English column than

these fierce Carbineers among the Dutch of the Pietersburg district. When they were disbanded many a Boer saw in the fact the hand of God, and thanked Him earnestly and took to the field with renewed hope. Few in their number they had been, those Carbineers, but bitter to meet, with their daring and their ruthlessness. Having no more Carbineers to fear,* in January the Boers began to assemble in force, and by the 22nd day of that month Commander Beyers had so many men that he fairly beleaguered the town of Pietersburg, with its garrison ; its High Court of Military Justice ; its Buccaneers on trial ; its prison full of them and of sturdy Boers captured in war ; and its " burgher camp," holding many women and children and 150 Boer men, kept as captives but with less stringent vigor than was the case with those held in gaol walls. No soldiers moved out of the town to drive Beyers back. It is indeed on record that the arm of the British was so weak then, that the officer in charge of a cow-gun (a heavy piece of field artillery drawn by bullocks, hence its name), refused to venture it out of the town lest it should be lost. The garrison sat down on its defences and let Beyers do what he willed.

On the night of January 22nd the Boers struck a blow, rushing some of the entrenchments, getting to the burgher camp and releasing the Boer men held therein. Scandalous rumors

---

*The operations of the Bushveldt Carbineers, it may be noted here, and those of Morant in particular, had been attended with a quite remarkable degree of success: and there do not seem to have been any special acts of brutality on Morant's part until the tragic events in the Spelonken district. This unofficial despatch, dated October, 1901. gives some idea of Morant's methods when in command of his first post. It is addressed to an officer of the Carbineers:-

9/5/'01. Styrdespoort.

Dear —.

Just an unofficial note to let you know my whereabouts. Midgely is 16 miles E. of me with a troop. I am 30 miles SS.W. of Pietersburg with another troop. Patrolling the country on d——d awful bits of horseflesh. But, with judicious nursing, I've got the horses a lot fitter and better than when they were supplied to us. On my way over from Pietersburg I heard of five Boers, armed, and in a very nasty position to attack, in a terraced kloof. As our horses then could hardly raise a walk, I should hardly have been able to snap them-certainly not without loss of some men ; so I came on into camp, reported them to Major Macdonald, of the Wilts here ; and, leaving camp at 3 a.m. next morning, we got the five. Surprised them at daybreak. Got 'em without any loss. Five Mausers and whips of ammunition. There are two other Boers reported about. With luck, we'll secure their scalps. As I said, our horses are greatly improved, but if you can get us better ones, for the Lord's sake do so. I'm using natives (Kaffir boys) as much as possible in order to save horseflesh. Midgely came over here from Chunespoort with a patrol, and camped the night last Monday. The men I've got here are VERY satisfactory. Eland is an excellent Sergeant, and the Afrikander troopers —especially Botha—are invaluable owing to their thorough knowledge of Dutch and Kaffir.

Yours obediently,

HARRY H. MORANT.

---

there be, that, on that night, soldiers who should have been guarding forts were tempted from their duty by the Boer women of the burgher camp, and that thus the task of the enemy was made easy. Such may be true, or may not. But certainly Beyers gained this great success, and there was consternation in the town, men not knowing what next might be done, and fearing much an enemy so bold and now so much reinforced. So great in truth was the fear, that those who were sitting in judgment on the malefactors of the Carbineers armed their prisoners, and brought them out of their cells to help fight for the lives and freedom of their gaolers. On the morning of January 23rd, very early, before the summer sun had shown the tip of a finger above the veldt, and only a faint shadow of white light in the East gave promise of the day, the Boer force came rushing on the town, and soldier and Buccaneer stood side by side to withstand the onset. Morant was in command at his own prison, and right gallantly he held himself, fighting like the brave man that he was, and having probably in his heart more hope than fear of death, since an evil fate threatened him just then so sorely. The others too, Lenehan, Picton, Handcock and Witton, showed out as men of courage.

Bushveldt Carbineer Officers in Camp.
With visitors from German Missionary Reuter's House.

In the end the Boers were beaten back. What other end could be, when they were confronted even by the very prisoners, willing to fight though in the shadow of the gallows? And the Buccaneers having fought a good fight went back to their cells : and the court-martial, a little wearied by its early morning fight, met as usual that day, and was a little more dour than usual with the accused, because when judges lack sleep it is hard for them to be good-tempered.

They be strange people these British! Many men, I take it, will not be able to forbear to think that it was a pity, aye a great pity, that Morant and Handcock and Witton and Picton were not, after that stern fight, given horse, and told to betake themselves away, after the enemy—to fall by their hands, in requital for their sins, or mayhap to escape to the Portuguese land. They were such doughty fellows, so brave to help their country, that the death of two of them by comrades bullets, and the chaining of a third in a prison of his own people seems against Nature, and pitiful, though in truth just.
Morant showed neither shame nor fear at his trial. He could not be got to see that he had done anything of wrong: he could not be got to whine and play the dastard. Openly admitting the

murders, he, with strange folly, pleaded custom of the war, and orders from headquarters as his excuse, swearing that he had had from the first orders from his superior officer to take no prisoners, and had been told that these orders came from the Commander-in-Chief. Whatever truth there might have been in the plea,* its folly was clear, for it was with the Commander-in-Chief that his final fate rested. One witness supported Morant's evidence in this regard. It was further urged by Morant that those whom he had killed were all notorious train-wreckers, or else had been concerned in the murder of Captain Hunt, and therefore deserved their fate. But there was no evidence to support this plea. As to his drum-head "court-martial" on Visser, that was brushed aside as illegal.

" Was your court-martial," asked Colonel Denny, who was presiding, " constituted the same as this? Was it carried on under the rules of the Army Act?"

"Was it the same as this this?" broke in Morant, looking at the glittering uniforms around. "No, it was not half so handsome. As to rules and sections, we had no Red-book ; and knew nothing of them. But, remember this : we were out fighting Boers, not sitting-comfortably behind wire fences. We got 'em and we shot 'em under Rule 303."

"Point 303" was the British rifle-calibre. The fierce retort, rude in its beginning, brutal in its ending, showed how little Morant was guided by good judgment in his attitude to the court.

More to the man's credit was the effort that he made to save his junior officers : " I alone was responsible," he said half a score of times. "You can't blame the young 'uns: they only did as I told 'em. They just carried out their orders, and that " —fiercely he spoke here— "they had to do. They obeyed my orders, and

---

* Lord Kitchener has since absolutely denied that any such order emanated from him.

thought they were obeying Lord Kitchener's. Captain Hunt told me not to bring in prisoners : He told me that they had said at headquarters that they didn't want prisoners to flood the concentration camps. I did not carry out those orders until my best friend was brutally murdered. Then I resolved to carry out orders. But if anybody is to blame it is me."

It was open to Morant either to hand in a statement or to give evidence on oath, on which he could be cross-examined. He elected to do the latter, but his cross-examination by Major Bolton, Provostmarshal of Pietersburg, was not a lengthy matter.

The uncompromising retorts of the accused were not to the relish of the counsel.

Bushveldt Carbineer Officers under arrest.

There was much sympathy, withal, for the accused among the judges. On the day that Morant and Handcock were found not guilty on the charge of murdering German missionary Hesse, two-members of the court-martial sent to them half-a dozen of champagne as a present. The night before the prisoners (still ignorant of their fate) were removed to Pretoria from Pietersburg, gaol regulations were relaxed, and they had a dinner, and drank together the golden liquor. It was Morant's last carouse.

In those cases where the verdict of the court-martial was one of guilty, and a sentence was passed, no hint of it was given to the accused. The sentences were sent on to Lord Kitchener, by him referred to the authorities in England, confirmed, and promulgated just 18 hours before they were carried into effect.

On February 21st the prisoners were ironed in Pietersburg gaol and entrained for Pretoria. As Morant held out his hands for the irons he cried : "This comes of Empire-building!" Some dismal forebodings must by this time have struck at the hearts of the prisoners, when they found themselves thus chained like felons.

On February 22nd Morant, Handcock, and Witton, were taken to Pretoria gaol. Lenehan was escorted to Capetown, and thence left for Australia; he was kept in ignorance of the fate of the others. There was no idea in his mind, or in that of any other of those concerned that an extreme penalty would be enforced. It would seem that there was fear in some minds of the Australian Government intervening on behalf of the condemned men; and it was desired to have them safely dead before such could happen. Major Thomas, who had acted as counsel for the accused, accompanied them to Pretoria, to watch over their interests.

On February 24th the prisoners and their counsel were informed that Morant and Handcock had been sentenced to death, and Witton to penal servitude for life. The death sentences were to be carried out on the following day. Morant took the news calmly: he had often faced death before, had in truth, often hoped for it. His dream of a better life was now definitely ended: after all, in sober thought, he perhaps mused, better death than to go back to the life of "The Breaker," with its hardships, its humiliations. In any case the man's splendid courage forbade him to show any fear.

To Major Thomas, however, the news was as a blow from a strong man. He had made himself the friend as well as the counsel of these brothers-in-arms from Australia. He could not imagine it possible that they would actually be shot; shot for what was seemingly being done every day, less flagrantly perhaps, but still done, and no word said. The Major rushed hot—foot to Lord Kitchener, and found that the Commander-in-Chief was away, would be away for a day or two ; and the chill thought came to his heart that the absence might have a motive. To the second-in-command at Pretoria, General Kelly, Major Thomas went, begging that the executions might not take place for a few days, until the King had been appealed to. His Majesty, he urged, would be certain to grant mercy. But General Kelly could hold out no hope—grant no reprieve. The sentences, he stated, had already been referred to England, and had been approved of by the authorities there. The men must die.

That was not the end of the efforts on behalf of the doomed men Morant and Handcock ; but all the steps that a most strenuous friendship could take were in vain. Major Thomas, at the close of the vain work, went back to the prisoners, feeling that it was because of the international aspect of the case that the ears of authority were deaf to all appeals; that to satisfy Germany the executions would have to be undertaken. That evening the prisoners looked out on the prison yard and saw there, two coffins.

On the morning of February 25, 1902, outside the walls of Pretoria, Morant (and with him Handcock) faced the sun for the last time. There were 18 men in the firing party. The morning was fair and clear. Morant scornfully refused a bandage for his eyes, and looked down the muzzles of the guns without fear. "Shoot straight," he said, "don't make a mess of it."

Australian fellow-soldiers who had failed to save their lives,- claimed the bodies of Morant and Handcock, and buried them in Pretoria cemetery. There "The Breaker " found his rest.

" Shoot straight! "

OBITER DICTA.

THE bodies of the executed officers were buried with but maimed rites. An eye-witness at Pretoria records that on the evening of the 25th he was walking out of the town when "just as I was passing the gaol a hearse drove through the gates with a group of soldiers and officers accompanying-about a dozen persons altogether. I followed the hearse to the cemetery and saw the funeral. The parson from the cathedral here met the coffins at the gate and led the party to a detatched portion of the ground, where a service took place after the bodies were lowered. The parson recited a preamble to the burial service : 'For as much as this is unconsecrated ground,' &c., &c., 'I proceed to dedicate this grave,' &c., &c., letting his hearers plainly know the difference between 'consecrated ground' and a 'dedicated grave.' Some of the service was omitted too. It was a mournful sight."

When the news reached Australia-which it did after more than a month's delay—the justice of the sentences was generally acquiesced in, though there was some dissatisfaction at the thought that the men had been shot "on the back-stairs," so to speak; that such stringent precautions had been taken to prevent any news of the charges, the trials, or the sentences reaching Australia; and that the widow of one of the executed men had been left in absolute ignorance of his end. The circulation of various atrocious stories, absolutely unjustified by any facts, as to the Bushveldt Carbineers, helped, however, to cloud over any discussion as to the unnecessary cruelty, and the doubtful motives which attended the course of justice.

Lieut. Witton, who was sentenced to penal servitude for life, is now in an English gaol at Gosport, having reached Southampton in April, on the transport Canada.

As to Morant's fate, the feelings which it excited in Australia were fitly expressed in these verses from a brother rhymer (" Mous quetaire ") :—

A Gaol-Wall Inscription.

———

A volley-crack, a puff of smoke
  And dead the Murderer grins ;
—Come, cover with the Charity-cloak
  That multitude of sins.
And though some blame and count it shame
  I won't withhold the tear
For the cold heart, the bold heart
  That ceased its beating here.

They say his debts he oft forgot,
  But one he settled up,
They say he used to drink a lot,
  —His last was a bitter cup.
And right or wrong, or weak or strong,
  I can't keep back the tear
For the Devil-heart, the revel heart
  That ceased its beating here.

I know he went from bad to worse,
  I know what ill he wrought,
But I have seen him on a horse,
  And heard of how he fought ;
And, fool or wise, I own my eyes
  Are troubled with a tear
For the rough heart, the tough heart
  That ceased its beating here.

A sorry life of drink and debt,
　　That finished with the shrift
Men give the murderer, and yet
　　Was his the singer's gift ;
A scrap of song 'gainst a world of wrong !
　　I know—but here's a tear
For the Crime-heart, the Rhyme-heart
　　That ceased its beating here.

Some heels may spurn "The Breaker's" grave,
　　Some mouths thereon may spit,
But some have owned to hands that gave
　　A wreath to even it;
And here's a meed of poor word-weed
　　Would fain express the tear
For that Other-heart, that Brother-heart
　　That ceased its beating here.

LETTER FROM MAJOR THOMAS.

THE following letter from Major Thomas, Counsel to the accused at the court-martials, was received in Australia in April. It gives an impression of the feeling at Pretoria among Australian officers there :—

Army Post Office, Pretoria, 27/2'02.

Dear —.

Have you heard the news—the awful news? Poor Morant and Handcock were shot this morning at 6 a.m. It has broken me up completely. The order was signed yesterday sometime, and Lord Kitchener immediately left town and could not he approached. There was no time to do anything, but directly I heard the decision I went to General Kelly (A.A.G.) and begged and entreated him to ask Lord Kitchener to defer the execution to enable me to cable to England to the King on behalf of the Australian people for mercy ; but he was obdurate, and said the order came from England, and practically said grave political trouble had been roused (apparently over the Hesse murder in particular). I begged especially for Handcock, who was merely present as a Vet. Lieutenant when Morant ordered the Boers to be shot for outrages. I pleaded his want of education and military knowledge and all that I could plead, but of no avail. Poor Handcock was right when he wrote two months or more ago: "Our graves were dug before we left the Spelonken." They were dug ; I see it all clearly now, and why. I know what I cannot write in this accursed military-ridden country. My God! Poor Handcock, a brave, true, simple man ; and Morant, brave but hot-headed. They took their sentence with marvelous braveness. Their pluck astounded all. Poor Handoock's only trouble was for his three children. Poor chap. My God ! what a cruel thing to shoot him. Edwards (Adjutant B.V.C.) and I were with them up to 8 p.m. last night. They are to be buried together in the cemetery this afternoon, and some trusty friends will attend. So will end another act of the Tragedy. Witton gets penal servitude for life ; Picton is reprieved and cashiered, and they both leave for England first transport : but I think Witton may be sooner or later released. Morant and Handcock were doomed—politically doomed — through the iniquities of the Court of Inquiry, the proceedings of which got to Germany, I believe.

This shooting of Handcock, an Australian, is a grave matter and will cause untold bitterness ; but if told let it be told in the right way.

I am full of bitterness. I cannot here express my feelings. But when the time comes, if I am spared, I will. I know all that I expect ever will be known, and I am too true an Australian to shirk plain speaking if need be. And need there will be, I think. What I resented was dragging out a lot of details unless it was essential. I did not contemplate a sudden and unappealable death sentence. I thought the absolute acquittal in the Hesse case would mean at most a term of penal servitude, which could be remitted later on.

But, though not guilty, Morant and Handcock have (lied over that case because our own (no *not our-own* altogether) people would have them convicted before a trial.

·   ·   ·   ·

I will soon follow to Australia. I feel quite broken up. It is too painful to write about.

Poor, brave fellows, nothing will worry them again in this world, and if there be another world, God will not think worse of them there than we do, surely. May they rest in peace.

Yours sincerely,

J. F. THOMAS.

MORANT'S CHARACTER AS A SOLDIER.

This was the sworn evidence at the court-martial of the Commander of the Bushveldt Carbineers, in regard to Morant's character as a soldier :—

"Lieutenant Morant came to South Africa as a Corporal in the South Australian Mountecl Rifles, at the beginning of this war. His C.O., Major Reade, C.B., informed me that Lieut. Morant had been requisitioned for, and had acted as a despatch rider for General French. His time of service being up with the South Australians, he returned to England. Early in 1901, Lt. Morant returned to South Africa, and I received a letter from Col. Mackay, S.O. to oversea colonials, recommending Morant for a Commission. Lieut. Morant came to Pretoria, and I got him his appointment about March, 1901. He served at Strydpoort, for some months in command, and I had very good reports of him from the O.C. Strydpoort, Major Macdonald, Wiltshire Regiment.

"When Captain Hunt joined the B.V.C., and took command of the Spelonken detachment, he asked particularly for Lieut. Morant, and I allowed Morant to go to him. Before Captain Hunt's death, Lieut. Morant had done very good work.

I know one occasion when he had taken out a patrol of 22 men, and brought back 19 prisoners, although certain of the commando had tried to out him off. Afterwards, when I was at the Spelonken, I sent him to capture Federal Commandant Tom Kelly, who was notorious in this district, and who was then reported about 150 miles from Fort Edward. Lieut. Morant did an excellent piece of work, captured Kelly, and what remained of his commando, bringing them to Fort Edward.

I should be quite satisfied to have entrusted Lieut. Morant first of all my officers, after Captain Hunt's death, with any difficult or arduous undertaking.

"Prior to joining the B.V.C., Lieut. Morant had, I believe, received a commission in the Transvaal Constabulary.

"I knew Morant previously in Australia, 12 years before he came to South Africa. He had the reputation of being the pluckiest of riders. If there was a bad horse to be ridden in a steeplechase, Morant was asked to ride him. From my previous knowledge of him, I was very glad to have him serving under me, as he was just the man for the work."

MORANT'S EARLY LIFE.

Since the printing of the earlier pages of this work, some interesting facts have been brought to light as to Morant's early career in Australia. Morant, it seems, was in Charters Towers in 1884, and he married there, though not under that name. He and his wife separated after a very short period of wedded life. Morant left Charters Towers after a horsebuying transaction not exactly creditable   a cheque, which he paid as purchase-money for two horses, was dishonored. In September, 1884, Morant went to Hughenden (Q.) ; he did a little work for the paper there, and offered to buy a partnership in it, cabling to a titled person in England for a large sum of money for that purpose. The money, apparently, did not come to hand, for the partnership transaction was not completed. Morant seems to have got into some trouble as to his board-bill at a local hotel. He, at any rate, left the place suddenly-for Winton. He was afterwards heard of droving for Emmeralda Station, and Was, later, at Cloncurry (Q.). That was the beginning, or nearly the beginning, of his Australian career: and is fairly typical of the rest of his life in this country.

LIEUTENANT PICTON.

Lieutenant Picton was in May deprived of the distinguished conduct medal which he received for conspicuous bravery at Bothaville. Though but 24 years of age Picton had seen much service previous to the Boer war, in Algeria and The Congo with the French Foreign Legion. In the Congo he fought and killed a French officer in a duel for speaking contemptuously of the English. He had to leave the regiment through it and returned to England. When Loch's Horse was formed in England, Picton was one of the first to join. About the time Roberts' column reached Bloemfontein, Picton, then a corporal, was attached as galloper to Colonel Ross' staff. Colonel Ross was in command of the 8th Mounted Infantry Corps. Picton was with him at the farmhouse at Bothaville when Ross was so badly wounded and Le Gallais killed, Picton being the only one in the house who escaped injury. It was for his gallant conduct and bravery on that day that he was mentioned in despatches and afterwards received the distinguished conduct medal. Colonel Ross' successor, Colonel Hickey, offered young Picton a commission. He refused it, but later accepted one in the Bushveldt Carbineers. He secured many important Boer prisoners and again earned a "mention" from his commanding officer. Picton was the great-grandson of the celebrated General Picton (Waterloo Picton), and it is a coincidence that he also was cashiered, but afterwards re-instated by the Iron Duke.

Picton not only lost his commission and his distinguished service medal, but also his war medal, to which is attached six fighting bars.

———

THE BUSHVELDT OPERATIONS.

THE account of the Bushveldt Carbineers' operations embodied in this Memoir of Harry Morant is compiled from trustworthy documentary evidence -to the almost absolute exclusion of the less reliable and often conflicting accounts of more or less genuine "eye-witnesses." The following version by a Bushveldt Carbineer trooper to the Melbourne ARGUS is printed because it gives some important facts about the corps before the period when Lieut. Morant joined it, and because it seems to have the impress of truth. Certain names are suppressed for obvious reasons. The account shows one important fact : that before Morant's arrival in the Spelonken district there were atrocities on the part of the British troops, and that after his arrival, *until the death of Captain Hunt,* there was a markedly humaner method of warfare. This is the account of ex-Trooper J. A. Heath :-

"I joined the Bushveldt Carbineers on the 16th April, 1901, at Cape Town, and left for Pretoria on the 22nd April, and arrived there on the 2nd May, and left on the 10th May for Pietersburg. I, with 19 others, then joined Colonel Wilson's column, and we were sent to act as scouts round the Watersberg district; the column was pursuing Commandant Beyers. I remained one month with the Scouts, and then Major Lenehan sent down word that we were to return to Pietersburg at once. We did so, and arrived there early in June, 1901. We stayed in Pietersburg four or five days, and then about 60 of us were sent to the Spelonken district. The officers in charge were Captain ——, Captain ——, and Lieutenant Handcock, and also a non-com. officer.

"On the 2nd July about 40 of us were warned for patrol, accompanied by the officers. When we had got out about half-a-mile six others and myself were warned to go as an advance guard, and were told by the non-com. officer that there were some Boers expected on the road, and that we were to 'take no prisoners,' and 'take no notice of the white flag,' as the Boers were to be shot. He told us that they were Captain——'s orders, and that they were to be carried out. We came up to the Boers, six in number. A few shots were exchanged, and then they hoisted the white flag, and our sergeant gave orders to cease firing. We took their rifles and ammunition from them, and the sergeant said, 'You know your orders,' and we shot them. This date was 2nd July, 1901.

"Captain——was arrested in October, 1901, for the murder of six Dutchmen, and there were also other charges of murder brought against him. The trial by court-martial was held at Pietersburg, in January, 1902. Captain——was honourably acquitted by the court-martial, and released in February, 1902. No charge was brought against the other captain, and he was never under arrest. Captain —— was not an Australian, and had never been in Australia. I do not know his defence, as I did not hear it, but gave evidence at the trial, as I was one of the firing-party.

"Captain Hunt, Lieutenants Morant, Picton, and Hannan joined the Spelonken detachment at the end of July, 1901, and Captain —— left, and went to Pietersburg. About a fortnight after, some prisoners were brought into camp, under Lieutenant Morant, and he was asked by Captain Hunt why he brought them, and was told that, if he brought in prisoners, he would have to keep them on his own rations. The prisoners were kept there for some time, and then sent to Pietersburg.

"Lieutenant Witton joined the Spelonken detachment at the beginning of August. On the 6th August Captain Hunt and a party of 17 men went out on patrol, and received information from the kaffirs that there were Boers at Viljoen's farm, and Captain Hunt decided to make an attack. This attack was made in early morning, in darkness, when the Boers were thought to be asleep, but they heard our men coming, and waited fo them. Captain Hunt gave orders to rush the house ; the signal to commence the attack was to be a shot from his rifle. No sooner was the signal given than the Boers opened fire. Captain Hunt fell wounded, and Sergeant Eland was shot dead. Our men returned a few volleys, but as the fire got too hot the men retired. Two hundred kaffirs accompanied the party, but ran for their lives when the first shot was fired, and knocked over some of our men in their flight. The men returned to the farmhouse at daylight, with the exception of one trooper, who had gone to Fort Edward for reinforcements. In the meantime the Boers had left the farm. Captain Hunt's dead body was found near a spruit about 20 yards from the farmhouse. It was stripped, and terribly knocked about. The neck was broken, and there was a heel mark on his forehead, between the eyes. Some of his clothes had been cut off him with a knife, and his flesh had been cut into. It was considered that he had been murdered, and I understood this was proved at the trial by Mr. Reuter, native missionary.

"The reinforcements arrived from Fort Edward next morning, under Lieutenants Morant, Witton, Handcock, and Picton, and they had been told by Captain — that they were going out to avenge Captain Hunt, and if they caught the Boers they were to get 'no quarter.' The Boers were pursued, and our men came up to them about 6 o'clock in the evening. They fled, leaving their waggons behind, and a Boer slightly wounded, named Visser.

"Lieutenants Morant, Handcock, Witton, Picton, and Hannah, and Sergeant-Major Hammett were arrested in October last. Morant and Handcock were charged with 13 murders, including a German missionary. Witton was charged with 9 murders, and Picton 1 murder. After the preliminary inquiry, Hannan and Hammet were released.

[The facts as to the trials and findings have been already published in this book]

"There was no evidence that Handcock had shot the missionary, other than that he left the fort on horseback after the missionary had passed. Mrs. Schiels (wife of a Dutch commander, who was a prisoner), Mr. and Mrs. Bristow, and Mrs. Schiels' two sons were witnesses for the defence, and swore that Handcock was at their place, 40 miles away.

"As to the other charges, it was admitted that the Boers were shot, but the defence was that it was done under orders. Lieutenant Morant took all responsibility as senior officer, and said that he gave the orders, which he maintained he had himself received from his superior officers.

"On the 2nd July we never knew Lieutenant Morant, and

had never seen him, and did not know there was such a man. There was no charge of looting at the court-martial. The Boers there had nothing to loot, as they were mostly hunters, and lived on what they shot and mealies that they stole from the kaffirs. As to the drink, there was very little drink where we were, and the officers in question and the men were seldom in camp.We were always on trek on the veldt, and the majority of the officers were teetotallers. I never saw Lieutenant Handcock and Witton take any drink anywhere. That certainly had nothing to do with the shooting. All the officers and men of the V.B.C. considered Lieutenant Witton entirely innocent, and I was surprised when I arrived in Victoria to find that he was still a prisoner. I was detained in Pietersburg during the whole of the trial as a witness."

HARRY MORANT'S VERSES

———

HARRY MORANT ("The Breaker"), in common with most men, had flashes of poetic thought: but he was, in no true sense of the word, a "poet," nor are any of his writings "poetry." He had a gift of breezy, graceful expression, a happy ear for rhyming music, and a varied fund of experience to draw upon. So his verses are always readable: they never reach to the depths of absolute doggerel: they sometimes come close to being poetry. The essential reason why Morant could never be a "poet" is that he had no capacity for deep feeling. His was a light-hearted, and, not to use the term too offensively, a light-fingered nature. It had no deep-planted springs. Throughout, from birth to death, his life was consistent, always reckless, thoughtless, aimless, loveless. A horse he could dote on, and break its neck if need be, and feel truly sorry for it afterwards: a mate he could cherish, and forget in a month if another friendly person happened along. That is not the nature for a poet. As to Morant's verses, they are; as I have said, never contemptible, sometimes very good. If he had been better educated, or if he had had enough in his mind of fixed purpose to have given them some "polish" before publication, they would probably have been much better. But he "dashed off" his compositions. The photographic reproduction of his last verse M.S. (written in prison) shows Morant's method: there is hardly an alteration in the "copy." His ear seems to have been so good that no revision for metrical purposes was necessary, and he was not the man to seek out with labor a more felicitious phrase, or a more suitable word than first occurred to him. Since the purpose of this volume is not to present to the public a new versifier at his best, but rather to give as faithful a picture as possible of the character of Harry Morant, there has been no effort made at a "selection" from "The Breaker's" verses. Most that are available are published, with the idea that each will give some new hint, or strengthen some old one, as to the personality of Harry Morant.

Transcription of the above poem on Page 88

Much—A Little While.

Love me little, love me long"—
Laggard lover penned such song;
Rather, Nell !—in other style—
Love me much, a little while!

If that ministrel ever knew
Maid so kissable as you
(Like you there was never such)—
He'd have written, "Love me much"

Other loves have passed away:
Springtimes never last alway!
'T will be better, will it not,
To think that once we loved " at lot "?

——————

At Last.

When I am tired, and old, and worn,
 And harrass'd by regret;
When blame, reproach, and worldlings' scorn
 On every side are met ;
When I have lived long years in vain
 And found Life's garlands rue,
Maybe that I'll come back again-
 At last - at last— to you !

When all the joys and all the zest
 Of youthful years have fled,
Maybe that I shall leave the rest
 And turn to you instead ;
For you, Dear Heart, would never spurn
 (With condemnation due !)
If, at the close of all, I turn
Homeward —at last-to you !

When other faces turn away,
   And lighter loves have passed ;
When life is weary, cold, and gray—
I may come back—at last !
   When cares, remorse, regrets are rife-
Too late to live anew-
   In the sad twilight of my life
I will come back—to you !

Beyond His Jurisdiction.

It was a, Western manager, and a language man was he,
Thus spoke he to the shed-boss : " Send The 'Rager' round to
me; I'll hie me to the office where I'll write his crimson cheque,
Bid him roll his dusty swag up, or I'll break his no-good neck."

So when the bell was ringing—when "smoke-oh!" time was o'er,
Says the shed-boss—" Mick, your services are wanted here no
more." Then " The Rager " hung his shears up, stepped from
the shearing floor. And went a-swapping swear words 'round
at the office-door.

For the boss began to language, and "The Rager" langua-
ged back ; Says "The Rager"— "There's my brother, can't you
give him, too, the sack?" "Your brother? D—n your brother !
Yes. send him 'round here, quick!" "That narks yez." Michael
answered—" he's a cocky down in Vic."

Requiescat!

Dying! in the sheltering shade
By the myall branches made, —
While the horse-bells clanged and tinkled far away across the plain;
The wan stars above were blinking
As old Pat Magee lay thinking
Of the places and the faces he would never see again.

That long trip, his life, was over,
And the grizzled, gaunt old drover
"Gives delivery"; hands his way-bill to his Owner up above.
Vlhether now a Heaven or Hell come,
Pat will find old mates to welcome—
Saints a few and sinners many 'mong the ones he used to love.

Lived his years, some five and fifty,
Neither over-wise nor thrifty!
Many times he went a bender from the sober ways and straight;
The man found in times of trouble,
That Pat's friendsliip was no bubble,
And he never wronged a woman nor "went back" upon a mate!

And the Boss of all the bosses
May be lenient to the losses;-
On the track that Paddy travelled there was bound to be a few ;
And p'r'aps He who pays the wages
Knows how weary were some stages,
And there'll be a big percentage p'r'aps allowed on coming through!

.   .   .   .

So we dug upon the 'Bidgee,
Fenced it round with stakes of gidgee,
Paddy's grave! for burial service Jack just whispered: "Rest his soul!"
Then next morning, heavy-hearted,
Got the nags up and departed;
Did what Pat had never done: *left his comrade in a hole!*

Last Night.

Last night, when the moon rose -round and white-
  Over the crest of the distant hill,
You sang your song to us there last night,
  When the sleeping world lay hushed and still.

Oh, why did the scented breezes shake
  The oak trees' foliage then? I vow
It was that the envious birds should wake
  And hear your song'neath the leafy bough!

They say, in this sunlit Southern land
  The birds thereof have been silent long;
Why they sing no more I understand-
  For you have stolen the wild birds' song.

Ah, I saw the bright stars wane——and swoon,
  And heard the murmurous night-wind sigh!
You sang your song—and the placid moon
  Trembled and paled in the soft grey sky.

You sang last night, and the saddened bird
  Away to her leaf-hid nestlings flew,
Knowing their music would ne'er be heard
  Since Heaven had given their songs—to you.

Concerning a Good Horsewoman.

"Earl Beauchamp is to be the successor of Lord Hampden in the Governorship of N.S.W. The Hampden dynasty has been popular. . . The Honorable Miss Dorothy Brand is an excellent horsewoman, and very few professional lady riders of the show-rings can give points to this Government House young lady in the matter of pluck and skill in the side-saddle. The Honorable Dorothy Brand has earned quite a reputation in the post-and-rail country which hounds run in N.S.W."—*Newspaper extract.*

So now the Brands
Seek other lands ;
Alack ! long ere they reach 'em
A fickle crowd
Will cheer as loud
For godly Governor Beauchamp.

'Twill be Hampden's lot
To be soon forgot,
Now an Earl is his successor ;
But the new-chum Earl
Will bring no girl
Like Dorothy Brand—Gocl bless her!

Then let it be known,
That all of us own
Since her dad to Australia brought her,
That there has not been,
Nor will there be seen
Another such Governor's daughter.

Yes! we all concur
(In respect to her
Ideas are not dividing)
There's no "seat " nor "hands"
Like Dorothy Brand's
When she goes out a-riding!

And each Australian,
And every alien,
Who rides as straight as he "oughter,"
Has been fain to yield
In the hunting-field
To the prowess of Hampden's daughter.

So, doff your "cady"
To this young lady !
Hooray—with your hat in your hand;
Australia's pride
Was the girl who could ride
Like the Honorable Dorothy Brand.

————

Who's Riding Old Harlequin Now?

They are mustering cattle on Brigalow Vale,
Where the stock-horses whinny and stamp;

And where long Andy Ferguson, you may go bail,
　　Is yet boss on the cutting-out camp:
Half the duffers I meet would not know a fat steer
　　From a blessed old Alderney cow;
Whilst they're mustering there I am wondering here—
　　Who is riding brown Harlequin now?

Are the pikers as wild, and the scrub just as dense
　　In the brigalow country as when
There was never a homestead and never a fence
　　Between Brigalow Vale and The Glen?
Do they yard the big "micks" 'neath the light of the moon?
　　Do the yard wings re-echo the row
Of stockwhips and hoof-beats? And what sort of loon
　　Is there riding old Harlequin now?

There was buck-jumping blood in the brown gelding's veins,
　　But, lean-headed, with iron-like pins,
Of Pyrrhus and Panic he'd plentiful strains——
　　All their virtues, and some of their sins.
'Twas pity, some said, that so shapely a colt
　　Fate should with such temper endow—
He would kick and would strike, he would buck and would bolt—
　　Ah! who's riding brown Harlequin now?

A demon to handle! a devil to ride!
　　Small wonder the surcingle burst:
You'd have thought that he'd buck himself out of his hide
　　On the morning we saddled him first.
I can mind how he cow-kicked the spur on my boot,
　　And though that's long ago, still I vow
If they're wheeling a piker no new-chum galoot
　　Is a-riding old Harlequin now!

I remember the boss—how he chuckled and laughed
    When they yarded the brown colt for me:
"He'll be steady enough when we finish the graft
    Aud have cleaned up the scrubs of Glen Leigh!"
I am wond'ring to-day if the brown horse yet live,
    For the fellow who broke him, I trow,
A long lease of soul-ease would willingly give
    To be riding brown Harlequin now !

"Do you think you can hold him?" old Ferguson said-
    He was mounted on Hornet, the gray ;
I think Harlequin heard him——he shook his lean head,
    And he needed no holding that day.
Not a prick from a spur, nor a sting from a whip,
    As he raced among deadwood and bough ;
While I sat fairly quiet and just let him rip—
    But who's riding old Harlequin now?

I could hear 'em a-crashing the gidgee in front
    As the Bryan colt streaked to the lead,
Whilst the boss and the workers were out of the hunt,
    For their horses lacked Harlequin's speed ;
The pikers were yarded and skies growing dim
    When old Fergie was fain to allow
"The colt's track through the scrub was a knocker " to him-
    But who's riding brown Harlequin now?

From starlight to starlight—all day in between,
    The foam-flakes might fly from his bit ;
But whatever the pace of the day's work had been
    The brown gelding was eager and fit.
On the pack-horse's back they are fixing at load
    Where the path climbs the hill's gloomy brow ;
They are mustering bullocks to send on the road,
    But—who's riding old Harlequin now?

In Such a Night.

A flood of moonlight from the sky,
   Where far stars faintly twinkle;
And, softened by the night-wind's sigh
   Is heard the horse-bell's tinkle.

Above—the drooping myall leaf ;
   Below—the fire-log glowing ;
And stately pines in swart relief
   Against the light sky showing

The massy bloodwoods sway and shake,
   The moon-steeped box-leaves glisten ;
And e'en the wild hawk's nestlings wake
   In wonderment to listen

To lullabies (more tuneful far
   Than any song of Morning !),
That night-wings sigh when moon and star
   The heavens are adorning.

Young hearts may know a music rare
   When Springtide dawns are breaking.
Whilst boughs are dew-gemmed everywhere
   And wanton birds are waking

But dusky Night ! —when hopes lie dead
   And summer dreams have faded,
When darkened are those lights which led
   Ere following footsteps grew jaded:

Her melodies the power possess,
  When days drag lone and dreary,
To lull the heart's own bitterness
  And soothe a soul world-weary.

———

A Note to Nell.

I watched the full harvest-moon springing,
  White-faced, o'er the rim of the hill,
And the soldier-birds homeward went winging
  While all for a moment was still.
Now round my camp crickets are cheeping,
  And yonder, in accents more harsh,
The bull-frogs, awakened from sleeping,
  Chant hoarsely their tunes in the marsh.

The pine in my camp-fire is cracking,
  The summer night gathers in soon,
Though a jackass, belated, is cackling
  At the placid white face of the moon;
On the sward the soft shadows are lying,
  Vague and dark as the moon-shadows do,
And gently the night-wind is sighing—
  And its sigh sets me sighing—for you!

As the tired bird at evening flies restward
  When the gay, garish daylight is done,
So the broken-up bushman hies westward
  When he's finished and paid for his fun.
Yes, it strikes one as rather a pity
  So many things chanced to go wrong,
Or I might have been yet in the city,
  Not hereabouts -singing this song!

Well ! this jingle I send you to tell you
   You still are "the dearest and best,"
And there's one fellow will not forget you
   When roving about in the West;
But the low-burning pine-log gives warning
   To end this (I write by its light),
There's a long stage to ride in the morning,
   So, Sweetheart, so-long—and Good-Night !

Short Shrift.

I can mind him at the start—
Easy seat and merry heart!
Said he, as he threw a glance
At the crawling ambulance :

"Some day I'll be on the ground
And the van will hurry round!
Doc. will gravely wag his head:
'No use now ! the poor chap's dead!'

Every man must, soon or late,
Turn up at the Golden Gate :
When we weigh in —you and I—
How can horsemen better die!"

On that sunlit steeple course
He lay prone beneath his horse,
Never more his pal may ride
By that gallant horseman's side.

"Reckless fool?" What matter, mate?
All his time he'd ridden straight-
Went (smashed 'gainst that wall of sod!)
Spurred and booted to his God.

Carve in stone above his head
Words that some old Christian said:
"Grace he sought, and grace he found,
'Twixt the saddle and the ground!"

The Austral "Light."

We were standing by the fireside at the pub. one wintry night,
Drinking grog and " pitching fairies" while the lengthening
hours took flight, And a stranger there was present, one who
seemed quite city-bred—There was little showed about him to
denote him "mulga-fed."

For he wore a four-inch collar, tucked-up pants, and boots of tan—
You might take him for a new-chum or a Sydney city man—
But in spite of cuff or collar, Lord! he gave himself away
When he cut and rubbed a pipe-full, and had filled his colored clay!

For he never asked for matches—although in that boozing band
There was more than one man standing with a matchbox in his hand;
And I knew him for a bushman 'spite his tailor-made attire
As I saw him stoop and fossick for a fire-stick from the fire.

And that mode of weed-ignition to my memory brought back
The long nights when nags were hobbled on a far North-Western track;
Recalled camp fires in the timber, when the stars shone big and bright
And we learnt the matchless virtues of a glowing gidgee light.

And I thought of piney sand-ridges! – and somehow I could swear
That this tailor-made young johnnie had at one time been "out there"!
And as he blew the white ash from the tapering, glowing coal—
Faith! my heart went out towards him for a kindred country soul!

The Good Things Which Remain.

Bluey the cattle-dog gammons asleep;
   The pine-sparks fly and the embers glow,
While the horse-bells ring and the crickets cheep,
   And the black ducks call in the swamp below.

Night-dews are drenching the tasselled grass;
   Away in the West the moon rides low;
And the bushman's wakeful fancies pass
   To the light-o'-love of a year ago.

"Cattle-dog Bluey, now what think you?
   Cunningest dog upon all the earth!
Wake, you schemer ! and answer true--
   Tell us what games are their candles worth?"

One eye opens, and two ears prick :
   "Not very many, boss ! " grins the dog,
"Sweethearing's vanity- best to stick
   To good tobacco and decent grog!"

————

The Brigalow Brigade.

There's a band of decent fellows
   On a cattle-run out-back-
You'll hear the timber smashing
   If you follow in their track;
Their ways are rough and hearty,
   And they call a spade a spade,
And a pretty rapid party
   Are the Brigalow Brigade.

They are mostly short of " sugar,"
  And their pockets if turned out
Would scarcely yield the needful
  For a decent four-man " shout !"
But they'll scramble through a tight place
  Or a big fence unafraid;
And their hearts are in the right place
  In the Brigalow Brigade.

They've painted Parkes vermillion,
  And they've colored Orange blue,
And they've broken lots of top-rails
  "Twixt the sea and Dandaloo ;
They like their grog and palings
  Just as stiff as they are made—
These are two little failings
  Of the Brigalow Brigade.

The Brigalow Brigade are
  Fastidious in their taste,
In the matter of a maiden,
  And the inches of her waist;
She must be sweet and tender,
  And her eyes a, decent shade——
Then her ma may safely send her
  To the Brigalow Brigade.

But woman, men, and horses
  With polo in between,
Are mighty potent forces
  In keeping purses lean:
But spurs are never rusty,
  Though they seldom need their aid—
For "the cuddies ain't too dusty "
  In the Brigalow Brigade.

Since the Country Carried Sheep

We trucked the cows to Homehush, saw the girls, and started back
W'ent west, through Cunnamulla, and got on the Eulo track,
Carnped awhile at Goorybibil—but Lord ! you wouldn't know
It for the place where you and Mick were stockmen long ago !

Young Merino bought the station, fenced the run and built a shed,
Sacked the stockmen. sold the cattle, and put on sheep instead ;
But he wasn't built for Queensland, and every blooming year
One hears of labor troubles when Merino starts to shear.

There are ructions with the rouseabouts, and shearers strike galore:
The like was never heard of in the cattle days of yore ;
Whilst slowly round small paddocks now the sleeping lizards creep—
And Goorybibil's beggared since the country carried sheep!

They've built bush yards on Wild Horse Creek, where in the
morning's hush We've sat silent in the saddle, and listened for
the rush Of the cleanskins—When we heard 'em it was "wheel 'em
if ou can," While gidgee, pine, and mulga tried the nerve of horse
and man !

The boys were after horses ere the starlight waned away—
The billy would be boiling by the breaking of the day ;
Whilst our horses—by "Protection"—were all in decent nick,
When we rode up the 'Bidgee where the cleanskins mustered thick.

The "mickies" that we've branded there ! the colts we had to ride !—
In Goorybibil's palmy days, before the old boss died ;
Could Yorkie Hawkins see his run, I guess his heart would weep—
For Goorybibil's beggared—since the country carried sheep !

From sunrise unto sunset through the summer days we'd ride-
And stockyard rails were up and pegged with cattle safe inside,
When 'twixt the gloaming and the dark we'd hear the welcome note

Of boist'rous, pealing laughter from the kookaburra's throat.
Camped out beneath the starlit skies—the treetops overhead,
A saddle for a pillow and a blanket for a bed,
'Twas pleasant, mate, to listen to the soughing of the breeze
And learn the lilting lullabies that stirred the nulga trees.

Our sleep was sound in those days, for the mustering days were hard—
The morrows might be harder, with the brandings in the yard !
But did you see the station now —the men ! and mokes ! they keep—
You'd own the place was beggared —since the country carried sheep !

———————

Stirrup Song.

We've drunk our wine, we've kissed our girls, and funds are getting low,
The horses must be thinking it's a fair thing now to go,
Sling up the swags on Condamine, and strap the billies fast,
And stuff a bottle in the bag, and let's be off at last.

What matter if the creeks are up —the cash, alas ! runs down—
A very sure and certain sign we're long enough in town ;
The local rides the "boko," and you'd better take the bay—
"Quartpot" will do to carry me the stage we'll go to-day.

No grass this side the Border fence, and all the mulga's dead ;
The horses for a day or two will have to spiel ahead ;
Man never yet from Queensland brought at bullock or a hack—
But lost condition on that God-abandoned Border track.

But once we're through the rabbit-proof, it's certain since the rain
There's whips of grass and water, so it's "West-by-North" again ;
There's feed on Tyson's country, we can "spell" the mokes a week
Where Billy Stevens last year trapped his brumbies, on Bough Creek.

The Paroo may be quickly crossed -the Eulo Common's bare-
And, anyhow, it isn't wise, old man, to dally there !
Alack-a-day ! far wiser men than you or I succumb
To woman's wiles and potency of Queensland wayside rum !

Then over sand and spinifex ! and on o'er ridge and plain,—
The nags are fresh ! besides, they know they're Westward bound again !
The brand upon old "Darkie's" thigh is that upon the hide
Of bullocks we shall muster on the Diamintina side.

We'll light our camp-fires while we may, and yarn beside the blaze;
The jingling hobble-chains shall make at music through the days ;
And while the tucker-bags are right, and we've at stock of "weed,"
The swagman will be welcome to a pipeful and a feed.

So fill your pipe, and, ere we mount, we'll drain a parting nip:
Here's now that "West by North" again may prove a lucky trip;
Then back once more, let's trust you'll find your best girl's merry face,
Or, if she jilts you, may you get—a better in her place !

————

Lost Light.

In starless night l heeded not
   The utter blank above ;
I dree'd a lonely, forlorn lot,
   Untouched nor cheered by Love.

A meteor shot across the sky,
   Brief blaze of dazzling light !-
And evermore aware was I
   How dreary was the night.

So life was blank before you crossed
  Its aimless, forlorn ways,
Thy Love flashed, star-like, and was lost,
  Save mem'ry of its rays.

Had heart ne'er stirred with love for you !
  Nor sight that meteor seen !—
Life's dreariness I never knew,
  Nor——what Life might have been !

———

Some Other Somebody.

Somebody's horse has finished his feed,
  Somebody's saddle is on ;
But never a local the tracks can read,
  Or know where Somebody's gone.

Over the rails and up the creek,
  As soon as the sun goes down:
How is it every night this week
  That Somebody's off to town?

Grass is dewy, and overhead
  Evening stars are bright ;
And startled wallabies hear the tread
  Of galloping hoofs at night.

Through the scrub and over the plain
  Somebody's galloping fast.
Never a pull on the bridle rein
  Till the town lights show at last.

Somebody's horse has whips o' work——
    Whips o' work of late——
Since Somebody's brown was seen in town
    Tied to Somebody's gate.

But the wherefore why Somebody rides,
    And the track that the brown horse goes,
Only his rider (and one besides :
    Some other Somebody) knows!

———

Kitty's Broom.

When Kitty glides into the room,
    There I contrive to stay
And watch her while she with her broom
    Sweeps all the dust away.

For bright-faced, slender Kitty's such
    A comely sight to see.
She grasps that broom with magic touch
    And waves it willingly.

And with her white and shapely arms,
    Where dimples love to play,
She wields that magic wand and charms
    Dull care—and dust—away.

All this life's care and sad concerns
    No longer darkly loom ;
All shadow into sunlight turns
    When Kitty "does" the room.

Along Life's thorny path of gloom
I'd wend a cheerful way
Did Heav'n send Kitty with her broom
To brush the briars away.

———

Butchered to Make a Dutchman's Holiday.

In prison cell I sadly sit——
A d—d crestfallen chappy!
And own to you I feel a bit-
A little bit—unhappy!

It really ain't the place nor time
To reel off rhyming diction;
But yet we'll write a final rhyme
While waiting cru-ci-fixion!

No matter what "end" they decide—
Quick-lime? or "b'iling ile?" sir!
We'll do our best when crucified
To finish off in style, sir!

But we bequeath a parting tip
For sound advice of such men
Who come across in transport ship
To polish off the Dutchmen!

If you encounter any Boers
You really must not loot 'em,
And. if you wish to leave these shores,
For pity's sake DON'T SHOOT 'EM!!

And if you'd earn a D.S.O.—
   Why every British sinner
Should know the proper way to go
   Is: ASK THE BOER TO DINNER!

Let's toss a bumper down our throat
   Before we pass to Heaven,
And toast : "The trim-set petticoat
   We leave behind in Devon.

[*The Last Rhyme and Testament of Tony Lumpkin,*— "THE BREAKER"]

———

"Just Like You."

He was a bachelor, gallant and gay,
   She was a spinster prim-
Pretty and prim, with a wonderful way
   Which had captivated him.

Now, he "really didn't know what to say !"
   So, never frigid nor freezy,
Molly Maginnis managed that day
   To make his contract easy.

"I guess that I'll get you a wife," said she ;
   "Find some kissable girl for you ;
Please to tell me the sort she must be :
   Shall her eyes be brown or blue ?
Shall she be of the 'plump and the pleasing sort'?
   Will the 'slender and willowy do' ? "

But here the bachelor, cutting her short,
   Said: "SHE MUST BE JUST LIKE YOU!
And to me, sweetheart, 'tis distinctly clear
   That—there's none in the world like you."

————

While Yet We May.

Ancient, wrinkled dames and jealous—
They whom joyless Age downcasts—
And the sere, gray-bearded fellows
Who would fain re-live their pasts—
 These, the ancients, grimly tell us :
"Vows are vain, and no love lasts."

Fleeting years fulfil Fate´s sentence,
Eyes must dim, and hair turn gray,
Age brings wrinkles, p´rhaps repentance ;
Youth shall quickly hie away,
And that time when youth has gone hence,
We—and love—have had our day.

Let the world, and fuming, fretting,
Busy wordlings pass us by,
Bent on piles of lucre getting—
They shall lose it when they die ;
Past and future, sweet, forgetting—
Seize the present ere it fly.

Your bright eyes are soft and smiling,
Pouting lips are moist and red,
And your whispers wondrous wiling—
Surely they would quick the dead—
And these hours they´re now beguiling,
All too hasty will have fled.

Years may bring a dole of sorrow,
Time enough to fast and pray,
From the present pleasures borrow,
Let the distant future pay ;
Leave the penance for the morrow,
Sweetheart, love and laugh to-day.

———

The Admiral !
(A long shot for the 95´ Cup.)

It was the time when punters ask-
  " What horse, think you, the Cup will win ?'"
And men essay the simple task
  Of doing surplus dollars in

Each horse´s breeding, age, and "weight,"
  I scanned ; then sought a pal of yore,
Whose tips were tolerably straight—
  He'd put me on "good things " before.

I found Gamaliel in the blues,
  Recovering from rum, alack !
I named the horses, bade him choose
  The likeliest - and best to back.

But he, the Oracle, seemed glum—
Sat sad and silent in his chair
Till half a tumblerful of rum
Produced a somewhat brisker air.

Then spake: "Hard times and biz. forlorn
Have changed these days from days of yore.
And Melbourne now, alas! is shorn
Of old Cup glories evermore.

We're stiff as biscuits here in town:
And all the chaps are 'up a tree'—
And more, the Cup— with stakes cut down—
Is not the race it used to be!"

He drained his glass and heaved a sigh,
And o'er the list of horses looked ;
Then, slyly, winked his dexter eye
And said, "I guess 'The Cup,' is *cooked*"

Another drink he drained. The same,
In lesser quantity, I took;
Whilst inspiration somehow came
From emphasis he laid on *"cook."*

"The horse that's owned by Sammy Cook?"
" Guessed well and wisely," said my pal ;
"Get hence, and with some honest 'book'
Put your 'bit' on—The Admiral."

The Admiral's the horse I'm "shook"
Upon; and for the Cup I shall
Place confidence in "Captain Cook"
And dollars on his—Admiral

By the Willows.

The sky was the softest shade of grays,
  Save Eastward, where gleamed one fire-edged cloud ;
I watched in the dawning the brown hills raise
  Their wood-clad crests from their misty shroud,
    As I waiting stood
    At the edge of the wood,
Where the river has wound through its waste of sand,
    And its broad Tide slips.
    By the thirsty tips
Of willow-trees fringing Fairyland.

Till you came, as the morning sunbeams came,
  And the whole of this fair world waxed more bright;
And the sunlight shone upon fields aflame,
  Where the valley was flooded with yellow light.
    And we dallied that day
    Till the skies waxed gray,
And the gloaming yielded to dusky night,
    For the hours had sped
    With stealthy tread,
As though Dark were jealous of Day's delight !

Years come and go, but they cannot efface
  What are mem'ries now of Fairyland—
Your innocent eyes and your girlish grace,
  And the soft warm clasp of your little hand.
    But I stand alone
    Where the sunlight's thrown
On the wllow-trees 'ere the day is done-

When their drooping fringe
Just borrows a tinge
Of fiery light from the fading sun.

Now a gray mist creeps o'er the rugged hill,
   And the birds which sung in the morn are dumb,
Whilst here by the willows I wait until
   That other, and longer, Night. shall come !
      There's a faint, faint plash
      And a silvery flash
Where the waters swirl round the willow stems,
      Whilst the purple sky
      Unfolds on high
Its wonderful spangle of golden gems

"Those who will of the asvogels hovering over stark bodies"

Notes:

Advertisements in the original book:

A Bagasse Fibrous Composition Panel.

100

Lightning Source UK Ltd.
Milton Keynes UK
UKHW02f1922230318
319970UK00027B/440/P